AIME Practice Tests
Volume 1

AlphaStar Academy
Math Development Team

© 2021 AlphaStar Academy. All rights reserved.

About AlphaStar Academy

AlphaStar Academy is an education company based in California. It offers extensive training programs for gifted students towards national and international Math and Science competitions such as American Mathematics Competitions, MATHCOUNTS, USA Math Olympiads, USA Computing Olympiads, and F=ma.

Students and teams from AlphaStar Academy performed extremely well in Mathematics competitions and olympiads, with countless students finishing in the top 10 and teams finishing in first place in competitions including Harvard-MIT Math Tournament, Princeton Math Competition, Stanford Math Tournament, Berkeley Math Tournament, and Caltech Harvey Mudd Math Competition. Dozens of AlphaStar Academy students got perfect scores in AMC 8/10/12 over the years and most of the MATHCOUNTS California team members in recent years were AlphaStar students. Moreover, every year between 2017 and 2020, at least one of the six-member USA IMO team were AlphaStar students/alumni.

Starting 2020, AlphaStar Academy has started offering all of its courses and programs online:

https://alphastar.academy/

About the Authors

This book contains four AIME practice tests with new problems and insightful solutions. The tests were originally written by AlphaStar/A-Star faculty several years ago. Since then lots of AlphaStar students took the tests. Using their results and data, the tests have recently been revised and improved by a team of AlphaStar Math developers with the goal of aligning the tests in terms of difficulty and style with the AIME exams of 2020's. Dr. Ali Gurel, AlphaStar Academy co-founder and Math Director, led the team and did the final editing.

Overall, at least 48 people contributed to various stages of this book. The authors and contributors participated and got excellent results in the American Mathematics Competitions sequence, other Math competitions, and Olympiads. Most of them qualified for the USA Mathematics Olympiads and 6 of them even participated in the International Mathematical Olympiads. We thank everyone involved in helping bringing this book to life which hopefully will help many students in their math journeys.

Contributors to writing problems and solutions:
Aaron Lin, Alex Song, Ali Gurel, Brian Shimanuki, Caleb Ji, Eugene Chen, Evan Chen, Joshua Sloane, Mehmet Kaysi, Omer Faruk Tekin, Richard Spence, Richard Yi, and Rick Huang.

Giving invaluable feedback, new insights, and improvements:
Aaron Lin, Alex Song, Ali Gurel, Andrew Lin, Caleb Ji, Edward Jin, Eugene Choi, Freya Edholm, Justin Stevens, Lazar Ilic, Mehmet Kaysi, Michael Choi, Richard Spence, Saranesh Prembabu, and Tomas Choi.

Math Development Team who wrote more problems, solutions, and edited the tests:
Aaron Chen, Adam Tang, Alex Gu, Ali Gurel, Alice Zhong, Andrew Chang, Andrew Wen, Aniketh Tummala, Dennis Chen, Edwin Xie, Ethan Lee, George Cao, Hanna Chen, Henry Wang, Jamin Xie, Jiakang Chen, Jieun Lim, Kelly Cui, Linus Tang, Michelle Wei, Nikhil Thakur, Olivia Xu, Robert Yang, Stephen Xia, Steven Pan, Tiger Che, and Zihongbo Wang.

To The Reader

The American Invitational Mathematics Examination (AIME) is a 3-hour, 15-question, short answer test taken in the USA and many other countries by thousands of pre-college students. The questions on the AIME are not straightforward and require a very deep level of thought, beyond textbook problems and basic formulas, in order to be solved.

Do not be discouraged by the difficulty of the problems and tests. These problems are meant to be challenging even to the strongest competitors. For example, the average score on an AIME is usually around 5 out of 15, and less than 3% of competitors correctly solve more than 10 of the problems. We have intended for these practice tests to be representative of recent AIME's and what we expect the actual contest to be like in the years to come. Some questions may be more difficult than those on a current, average-level AIME, in order to ensure that you are prepared for potential harder questions.

We have put in our best efforts to create high quality practice tests and help improve your skills. In order to use the book most effectively, you should try to simulate an actual testing environment, attempting to solve each test within the 3-hour time limit. However, if you are at first unable to finish all the problems within the time limit, you are strongly encouraged to continue working and attempt all the problems on the test before reading the solutions. We tried to present the ideas and solutions in an intuitive way, showing the reasons behind the steps that we are taking. When you read the solutions, try to understand the motivation behind them, so that you can adopt and apply these ideas yourself in the future to other problems. For many of the solutions we gave alternate solutions showing that there are usually several ways to solve a problem. If you think the problem might have another solution that is simpler or more elegant, challenge yourself to find one. When you do find such solutions, it will give you more self-confidence as well as great joy.

Have challenging and inspiring goals and keep working hard to achieve them while enjoying the journey of problem-solving.

Table of Contents

AIME PRACTICE TESTS VOL 1

TEST-1

INSTRUCTIONS

1. This test has 15 questions. All answers are integers ranging from 0 to 999, inclusive. Your score will be the number of correct answers; i.e., there is neither partial credit nor a penalty for wrong answers.

2. No aids other than scratch paper, graph paper, ruler, compass, and protractor are permitted. In particular, calculators are **not** permitted.

3. Figures are not necessarily drawn to scale.

4. You will have **3 hours** to complete the test.

2

1. In the city of Metroville, there is a 10% chance it will rain Monday, a 30% chance it will rain Tuesday, and a 20% chance it will rain Wednesday. Given that the events of rain on Monday, Tuesday, and Wednesday are independent of each other, there is a $p\%$ chance that it will rain on at least two of the three days. Find $10p$.

2. Let S be the set of positive integers that cannot be written in the form $5a + 7b$ for non-negative integers a and b. Find the sum of the elements of S.

3. Let a and b be positive integers such that $\log_2(b^a) = 40960$ and $\log_2(a^b) = 12288$. Find the value of $\log_2(a^2 b)$.

4. Adam writes a fourth degree polynomial $P(x) = (x^2 + ax + b)(x^2 + bx + a)$ on a board, where a and b are different real numbers. He notes that both 2 and 3 are roots of $P(x)$. If the sum of all distinct possible values of $|b|$ is $\frac{m}{n}$ where m and n are relatively prime positive integers, find $m + n$.

5. $ABCD$ is a trapezoid with $\overline{AB} \parallel \overline{CD}$. Diagonals $\overline{AC}$ and $\overline{BD}$ intersect at E. Let L and M be points on segments $\overline{AD}$ and $\overline{BC}$, respectively, so that $\overline{LM}$ is parallel to $\overline{AB}$ and contains the point E. Triangles ABE and CDE have areas 9 and 16, respectively. The area of trapezoid $ABML$ can be written as $\frac{m}{n}$ where m and n are relatively prime positive integers. Find $m + n$.

6. For a real number x, let $\lfloor x \rfloor$ denote the greatest integer not exceeding x. Find the value of

$$\sum_{k=0}^{72} \lfloor 1000 \cos(5k°) \rfloor.$$

7. Let $ABCD$ be a convex quadrilateral whose diagonals AC and BD intersect at P. It is given that $AD = 18$, $PD = 11$, $PB = 19$, and $\angle ADC = \angle ACD = 90° - \angle DBC$. Find AP^2.

8. Let $0 < \theta < 90°$ satisfy $\cos\theta = \frac{3}{5}$. The value of the infinite sum

$$\sum_{k=1}^{\infty} \frac{\sin(k\theta)}{2^{k-1}}$$

equals $\frac{m}{n}$ where m and n are relatively prime positive integers. Find $m + n$.

9. Let ABC be a triangle with side lengths $AB = 3$, $BC = 4$, and $CA = 5$. Let M be the midpoint of $\overline{CA}$. Let P be the circumcenter of triangle AMB and let Q be the circumcenter of triangle CMB. Let R be the circumcenter of triangle PMQ. The length of segment BR can be written as $\frac{p}{q}$ where p and q are relatively prime positive integers. Find $p + q$.

10. Let N be the number of nonempty subsets $S \subseteq \{1, 2, \ldots, 15\}$ such that S has no subsets of the form $\{n, 2n\}$ or $\{n, 2n + 1\}$ for any integer n. Find the remainder when N is divided by 1000.

11. The sequence $\{x_i\}$ satisfies $x_1 = \frac{1}{3}$ and $x_{n+1} = x_n^2 + x_n$ for all $n \geq 1$. Determine the value of

$$\left\lfloor \frac{x_1}{1 + x_1} + \frac{x_2}{1 + x_2} + \frac{x_3}{1 + x_3} + \cdots + \frac{x_{1000}}{1 + x_{1000}} \right\rfloor.$$

For a real number x, $\lfloor x \rfloor$ denotes the largest integer less than or equal to x.

12. Find the number of ways to color the squares of a 8×8 checkerboard with red and blue such that every 2×2 sub-square contains exactly two red squares. Rotations and reflections are considered distinct.

13. The numbers $1, 2, 3, \ldots, 100$ are written on a blackboard. Every second for 20 seconds, Carl selects three numbers a, b, c on the board such that $a + b + c$ is also on the board, erases all four numbers, and writes down $a + b$, $b + c$, and $c + a$ instead. After 20 seconds, the reciprocals of the numbers remaining on the board are the roots of the polynomial

$$x^{80} + a_{79} x^{79} + \ldots + a_2 x^2 + a_1 x + a_0.$$

What is the sum of all distinct prime factors of $\frac{a_2}{a_0}$?

14. Acute triangle ABC has orthocenter H and side length $BC = 12$. Denote M and N as the midpoints of $\overline{BH}$ and $\overline{CH}$. If the circumcircle of $\triangle HMN$ is tangent to the circumcircle of $\triangle ABC$, and $\tan \angle BAC = 7$, then the area of $\triangle ABC$ can be expressed in the form $\frac{p}{q}$ where p and q are relatively prime positive integers. Find $p + q$.

15. At Hilbert High School, 1000 lockers are arranged in a circle and numbered $1, 2, \ldots, 1000$ in that order. Each locker can be in one of three states: locked, unlocked (but closed) or open. Cindy begins by going around and playing with the lockers. When she visits a locker, she unlocks it if is locked, opens it if it is unlocked, and locks it if it is open. Initially all of them are locked. During her first trip, Cindy visits all the lockers starting with locker 1, unlocking them until she gets back to locker 1 (which is left unlocked but not opened yet). Then, Cindy visits lockers $1, 3, 5$, and so on, opening them until she returns to locker 1 (which is left open). Next, Cindy visits every third locker $1, 4, 7, \ldots, 997, 1000, 3, 6, 9, \ldots, 996, 999, 2, 5, \ldots, 998$ (in other words, every locker), locking each open locker and opening each unlocked one. Cindy continues this procedure, visiting every fourth locker, fifth locker, and so on, always starting and ending at locker 1. After her 1000th trip, how many lockers are locked?

Test-1 Answer Key

1. 98

2. 114

3. 34

4. 77

5. 142

6. 968

7. 115

8. 29

9. 221

10. 305

11. 997

12. 510

13. 271

14. 115

15. 370

Test-1 Solutions

1. In the city of Metroville, there is a 10% chance it will rain Monday, a 30% chance it will rain Tuesday, and a 20% chance it will rain Wednesday. Given that the events of rain on Monday, Tuesday, and Wednesday are independent of each other, there is a $p\%$ chance that it will rain on at least two of the three days. Find $10p$.

Answer (98): The probability that it rains on both Monday and Tuesday is $\frac{3}{100}$; that it rains on both Monday and Wednesday is $\frac{2}{100}$; that it rains on both Tuesday and Wednesday is $\frac{6}{100}$. However, we have over-counted the case where it rains on all three days an extra two times (occurring with probability $\frac{6}{1000}$). Thus,

$$p\% = \frac{3}{100} + \frac{2}{100} + \frac{6}{100} - 2 \cdot \frac{6}{1000} = \frac{98}{1000} = 9.8\%.$$

So p is 9.8 and $10p = 98$.

Alternate Solution: There are four desired cases: Three cases where it rains on two days but not the third day, and one case where it rains on all three days.

The probability that it rains on:

- Tuesday and Wednesday but not Monday is $0.9 \times 0.2 \times 0.3 = 0.054$.

- Monday and Wednesday but not Tuesday is $0.1 \times 0.8 \times 0.3 = 0.024$.

- Monday and Tuesday but not Wednesday is $0.1 \times 0.2 \times 0.7 = 0.014$.

- all three days is $0.1 \times 0.2 \times 0.3 = 0.006$.

Therefore, the desired probability is

$$0.054 + 0.024 + 0.014 + 0.006 = 0.098 = 9.8\%,$$

and the answer is $10 \times 9.8 = 98$.

2. Let S be the set of positive integers that cannot be written in the form $5a + 7b$ for non-negative integers a and b. Find the sum of the elements of S.

Answer (114): We use the process of elimination. First, place all non-negative integers into a table with five columns based on their values mod 5. Then, box the first multiples of 7 in each column, and finally, cross out these boxed numbers, as well as any number below them:

0	1	2	3	4
5	6	7	8	9
10	11	12	13	14
15	16	17	18	19
20	21	22	23	24
25	26	27	28	29
⋮	⋮	⋮	⋮	⋮

S is the numbers left in the table that are not crossed out. We find that

$$S = \{1, 2, 3, 4, 6, 8, 9, 11, 13, 16, 18, 23\}.$$

The sum of the elements in S is 114.

Alternate Solution: By the Chicken McNugget Theorem, the largest integer that cannot be written in the form $5a + 7b$ for non-negative integers a and b is $5 \times 7 - 5 - 7 = 23$. By checking all positive integers less than or equal to 23, we find the same set S as before.

3. Let a and b be positive integers such that $\log_2(b^a) = 40960$ and $\log_2(a^b) = 12288$. Find the value of $\log_2(a^2b)$.

Answer (34): Rewriting the given equations without the logarithms, we get

$$b^a = 2^{40960} \quad \text{and} \quad a^b = 2^{12288}.$$

Since a and b are positive integers, they must both be powers of 2. Let $a = 2^m$ and $b = 2^n$. The equations above reduce to

$$n \cdot 2^m = 40960 = 2^{13} \cdot 5 \quad \text{and} \quad m \cdot 2^n = 12288 = 2^{12} \cdot 3.$$

Note that from the left equation, n must be 5 times a power of 2. Trying $n = 5$ does not lead to a solution. Trying $n = 10$ gives $m = 12$. When $n = 20$ or more, $m \cdot 2^n$ becomes larger than $2^{12} \cdot 3$. So, the only solution is $(m, n) = (12, 10)$. The answer is $\log_2\left(a^2 b\right) = 2m + n = 34$.

4. Adam writes a fourth degree polynomial $P(x) = (x^2 + ax + b)(x^2 + bx + a)$ on a board, where a and b are different real numbers. He notes that both 2 and 3 are roots of $P(x)$. If the sum of all distinct possible values of $|b|$ is $\frac{m}{n}$ where m and n are relatively prime positive integers, find $m + n$.

Answer (77): Let $Q(x) = x^2 + ax + b$ and $R(x) = x^2 + bx + a$. We will do case work based on which polynomials 2 and 3 are roots of:

If 2 and 3 are both roots of $Q(x)$, then $Q(x) = (x - 2)(x - 3) \implies b = 6$.

If 2 and 3 are both roots of $R(x)$, then $R(x) = (x - 2)(x - 3) \implies b = -5$.

If 2 is a root of $Q(x)$ and 3 is a root of $R(x)$, then we have

$$Q(2) = 4 + 2a + b = 0 \quad \text{and} \quad R(3) = 9 + 3b + a = 0.$$

Solving this system of two equations yields $a = -\frac{3}{5}$ and $b = -\frac{14}{5}$.

Swapping the roles of $Q(x)$ and $R(x)$ symmetrically yields $a = -\frac{14}{5}$ and $b = -\frac{3}{5}$. Therefore, our desired sum is

$$\sum |b| = |6| + |-5| + \left|-\frac{14}{5}\right| + \left|-\frac{3}{5}\right| = \frac{72}{5}.$$

The answer is $72 + 5 = 77$.

5. $ABCD$ is a trapezoid with $\overline{AB} \parallel \overline{CD}$. Diagonals $\overline{AC}$ and $\overline{BD}$ intersect at E. Let L and M be points on segments $\overline{AD}$ and $\overline{BC}$, respectively, so that $\overline{LM}$ is parallel to $\overline{AB}$ and contains the point E. Triangles ABE and CDE have areas 9 and 16, respectively. The area of trapezoid $ABML$ can be written as $\frac{m}{n}$ where m and n are relatively prime positive integers. Find $m + n$.

Answer (142):

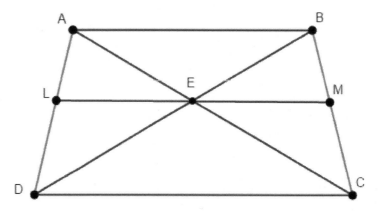

We will write the area $[ABML]$ as $[ABE] + [ALE] + [BME]$.

Since $ABCD$ is a trapezoid, $\triangle ABE \sim \triangle CDE$. The ratio of the areas is 9 to 16, so the ratio of the lengths is 3 to 4. In particular, $\frac{AE}{EC} = \frac{3}{4}$.

Then

$$[AED] = [CED] \cdot \frac{AE}{EC} = 16 \cdot \frac{3}{4} = 12.$$

Next, since $LE \parallel DC$,

$$\frac{AL}{AD} = \frac{AE}{AC} = \frac{3}{7}.$$

Using this, we find that

$$[ALE] = \frac{[AL]}{[AD]} \cdot [AED] = \frac{3}{7} \cdot 12 = \frac{36}{7}.$$

Similarly, $[BME]$ is also $\frac{36}{7}$. Finally,

$$[ABML] = 9 + 2 \cdot \frac{36}{7} = \frac{135}{7}.$$

The answer is $135 + 7 = 142$.

Remark: In general, for any trapezoid $ABCD$, it is true that

$$LE = ME \quad \text{and} \quad [ALE] = [BME].$$

The first equation, $LE = ME$, follows from

$$\frac{LE}{DC} = \frac{AL}{AD} = \frac{BM}{BC} = \frac{ME}{CD}.$$

To get $[ALE] = [BME]$, note that $\triangle ALE$ and $\triangle BME$ have the same height since $LM \parallel AB$.

6. For a real number x, let $\lfloor x \rfloor$ denote the greatest integer not exceeding x. Find the value of

$$\sum_{k=0}^{72} \lfloor 1000 \cos(5k^\circ) \rfloor.$$

Answer (968): Motivated by the fact that $\cos(\theta) = -\cos(\theta + 180^\circ)$, we pair the terms as follows:

$$\lfloor 1000 \cos 0^\circ \rfloor + \sum_{k=1}^{36} \left(\lfloor 1000 \cos(5k^\circ) \rfloor + \lfloor 1000 \cos(5k^\circ + 180^\circ) \rfloor \right)$$

$$= 1000 + \sum_{k=1}^{36} \left(\lfloor 1000 \cos(5k^\circ) \rfloor + \lfloor -1000 \cos(5k^\circ) \rfloor \right)$$

$$= 1000 + 2 \cdot \sum_{k=1}^{18} \left(\lfloor 1000 \cos(5k^\circ) \rfloor + \lfloor -1000 \cos(5k^\circ) \rfloor \right).$$

In the last equation above, we used $\cos(5(36 - k)^\circ) = -\cos(5k^\circ)$.

Note that for a real number r, the sum $\lfloor r \rfloor + \lfloor -r \rfloor$ is 0 if r is an integer and -1 otherwise.

So, in the sum above, aside from 1000, the only contributions come from the terms where $1000 \cos(5k^\circ)$ is not an integer. Using the following lemma, we will see that $1000 \cos(5k^\circ)$ is irrational (hence not an integer) for all the terms except for $k = 12$ and 18.

Lemma: Let $\alpha \in \{5^\circ, 10^\circ, \ldots, 90^\circ\}$. Then $\cos \alpha$ is rational only when α is 60° or 90°.

Proof. Let α be an angle such that $\cos(3\alpha)$ is irrational. Using the equation

$$\cos(3\alpha) = 4(\cos \alpha)^3 - 3 \cos \alpha$$

and the identities $\cos(180^\circ \pm 3\alpha) = -\cos(3\alpha)$ and $\cos(360^\circ - 3\alpha) = \cos(3\alpha)$, it follows that $\cos \alpha$, $\cos(60^\circ \pm \alpha)$, and $\cos(120^\circ - \alpha)$ are all irrational.

It is,
$$\cos(3\alpha) \notin \mathbb{Q} \Rightarrow \cos \alpha \notin \mathbb{Q}, \ \cos(60^\circ \pm \alpha) \notin \mathbb{Q}, \ \cos(120^\circ - \alpha) \notin \mathbb{Q}.$$
Starting with $\cos 45^\circ \notin \mathbb{Q}$ and $\cos 30^\circ \notin \mathbb{Q}$, we get the following:

$$\cos \mathbf{45}^\circ \notin \mathbb{Q} \Rightarrow \cos \mathbf{15}^\circ \notin \mathbb{Q}, \ \cos \mathbf{75}^\circ \notin \mathbb{Q}, \ \cos 105^\circ \notin \mathbb{Q}$$
$$\cos 105^\circ \notin \mathbb{Q} \Rightarrow \cos \mathbf{35}^\circ \notin \mathbb{Q}, \ \cos \mathbf{25}^\circ \notin \mathbb{Q}, \ \cos \mathbf{85}^\circ \notin \mathbb{Q}$$
$$\cos \mathbf{15}^\circ \notin \mathbb{Q} \Rightarrow \cos \mathbf{5}^\circ \notin \mathbb{Q}, \ \cos \mathbf{55}^\circ \notin \mathbb{Q}, \ \cos \mathbf{65}^\circ \notin \mathbb{Q}$$
$$\cos \mathbf{30}^\circ \notin \mathbb{Q} \Rightarrow \cos \mathbf{10}^\circ \notin \mathbb{Q}, \ \cos \mathbf{50}^\circ \notin \mathbb{Q}, \ \cos \mathbf{70}^\circ \notin \mathbb{Q}$$

14

It is left to check that $\cos 80°$, $\cos 40°$, and $\cos 20°$ are irrational.

Using the cosine double angle formula: $\cos(2\alpha) = 2(\cos\alpha)^2 - 1$, we conclude that if $\cos(2\alpha)$ is irrational, so is $\cos\alpha$. So it suffices to check the irrationality of only $\cos 80°$.

Let $y = \cos 80°$. We know that

$$\cos 240° = 4y^3 - 3y = -\frac{1}{2}.$$

So, $8y^3 - 6y + 1 = 0$. Replacing $2y$ by z we get $z^3 - 3z + 1 = 0$. By the Rational Root Theorem, the only possible roots of this polynomial are ± 1. But they don't satisfy the equation, so there is no rational root. Hence $\cos 80°$ is irrational. This finishes the proof of the Lemma.

Going back to the sum

$$1000 + 2 \cdot \sum_{k=1}^{18} \left(\lfloor 1000\cos(5k°) \rfloor + \lfloor -1000\cos(5k°) \rfloor \right),$$

we see that the terms $k = 12$ and 18 do not give a contribution since they make $1000\cos(5k°)$ an integer but by the Lemma above, all the remaining k values give a contribution of -1. The answer is then

$$1000 - 2 \cdot 16 = 968.$$

Remark: The lemma above is a special case of Niven's Theorem which states that the only rational values of θ in the interval $0 \le \theta \le 90$ for which $\sin\theta°$ is also a rational number are: $\theta = 0$, 30, and 90.

7. Let $ABCD$ be a convex quadrilateral whose diagonals AC and BD intersect at P. It is given that $AD = 18$, $PD = 11$, $PB = 19$, and $\angle ADC = \angle ACD = 90° - \angle DBC$. Find AP^2.

Answer (115):

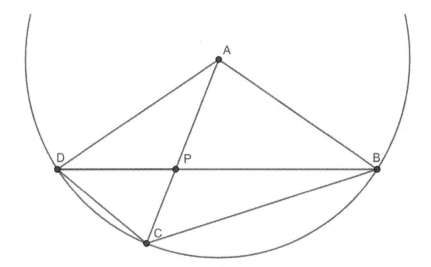

The conditions imply that $AD = AC = 18$ and that $\angle DBC = \frac{1}{2}\angle DAC$, so B lies on a circle centered at A passing through C, D. By Power of a Point, we have

$$18^2 - AP^2 = PD \cdot PB = 11 \cdot 19.$$

Hence $AP^2 = 324 - 209 = 115$.

8. Let $0 < \theta < 90°$ satisfy $\cos\theta = \frac{3}{5}$. The value of the infinite sum

$$\sum_{k=1}^{\infty} \frac{\sin(k\theta)}{2^{k-1}}$$

equals $\frac{m}{n}$ where m and n are relatively prime positive integers. Find $m + n$.

Answer (29): The geometric series involving $\sin(k\theta)$ and exponential term, 2^{k-1}, suggest using complex numbers. Using $\sin(k\theta) = \text{Im}(e^{ik\theta})$ and letting $\omega = \frac{e^{i\theta}}{2} = \frac{3+4i}{10}$, the summation reduces to

$$\sum_{k=1}^{\infty} \frac{\text{Im}(e^{ik\theta})}{2^{k-1}} = \text{Im}\left(\sum_{k=1}^{\infty} \frac{e^{ik\theta}}{2^{k-1}}\right) = 2 \cdot \text{Im}\left(\sum_{k=1}^{\infty} \frac{e^{ik\theta}}{2^k}\right)$$

$$= 2 \cdot \text{Im}\left(\sum_{k=1}^{\infty} \omega^k\right) = 2 \cdot \text{Im}\left(\frac{\omega}{1-\omega}\right)$$

$$= 2 \cdot \text{Im}\left(\frac{3+4i}{7-4i}\right) = 2 \cdot \text{Im}\left(\frac{5+40i}{65}\right)$$

$$= 2 \cdot \text{Im}\left(\frac{1+8i}{13}\right) = \frac{16}{13}.$$

16

The answer is $16 + 13 = 29$.

Alternate Solution: We set

$$S = \sum_{k=1}^{\infty} \frac{\sin(k\theta)}{2^{k-1}} \quad \text{and} \quad C = \sum_{k=1}^{\infty} \frac{\cos(k\theta)}{2^{k-1}}.$$

Using sine and cosine addition formulas gives

$$\frac{3}{5}S + \frac{4}{5}C = S\cos\theta + C\sin\theta$$

$$= \sum_{k=1}^{\infty} \frac{\cos\theta \sin(k\theta)}{2^{k-1}} + \sum_{k=1}^{\infty} \frac{\sin\theta \cos(k\theta)}{2^{k-1}}$$

$$= \sum_{k=1}^{\infty} \left[\frac{\cos\theta \sin(k\theta) + \sin\theta \cos(k\theta)}{2^{k-1}} \right]$$

$$= \sum_{k=1}^{\infty} \left[\frac{\sin((k+1)\theta)}{2^{k-1}} \right]$$

$$= \sum_{k=2}^{\infty} \left[\frac{\sin(k\theta)}{2^{k-2}} \right]$$

$$= 2(S - \sin\theta)$$

$$= 2S - \frac{8}{5}.$$

Similarly,

$$\frac{3}{5}C - \frac{4}{5}S = C\cos\theta - S\sin\theta$$

$$= \sum_{k=1}^{\infty} \frac{\cos\theta \cos(k\theta)}{2^{k-1}} - \sum_{k=1}^{\infty} \frac{\sin\theta \sin(k\theta)}{2^{k-1}}$$

$$= \sum_{k=1}^{\infty} \left[\frac{\cos\theta \cos(k\theta) - \sin\theta \sin(k\theta)}{2^{k-1}} \right]$$

$$= \sum_{k=1}^{\infty} \left[\frac{\cos((k+1)\theta)}{2^{k-1}} \right]$$

$$= \sum_{k=2}^{\infty} \left[\frac{\cos(k\theta)}{2^{k-2}} \right]$$

$$= 2(C - \cos\theta)$$

$$= 2C - \frac{6}{5}.$$

Solving this system of equations then gives $S = \frac{16}{13}$, for a final answer of 29, as desired.

9. Let ABC be a triangle with side lengths $AB = 3$, $BC = 4$, and $CA = 5$. Let M be the midpoint of $\overline{CA}$. Let P be the circumcenter of triangle AMB and let Q be the circumcenter of triangle CMB. Let R be the circumcenter of triangle PMQ. The length of segment BR can be written as $\frac{p}{q}$ where p and q are relatively prime positive integers. Find $p + q$.

Answer (221):

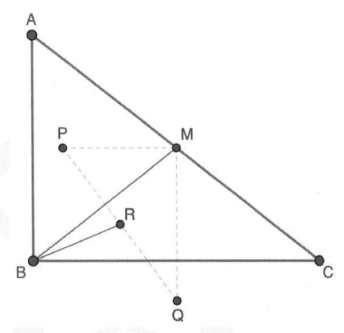

Firstly, note that PM bisects $\angle AMB$ and QM bisects angle $\angle BMC$ because triangles AMB and BMC are isosceles. Then, we have that $\angle PMQ$ is right. Thus, R is simply the midpoint of PQ.

Since P is the circumcenter of AMB and Q is the circumcenter of BMC, both P and Q lie on the perpendicular bisector of BM and B is the reflection of M over PQ. Thus, $\angle PBQ$ is also right. Doing some angle chasing, we get

$$\angle BPQ = \angle QPM = 90° - \angle PMB = 90° - \angle AMP = \angle BAC.$$

Hence, $\triangle PBQ \sim \triangle ABC$.

Let the ratio of similarity be x; that is, let $PQ = 5x$. Then, BM is simply twice the altitude of triangle PBQ, which is $\frac{24x}{5}$. However, BM is also $\frac{5}{2}$, so $x = \frac{25}{48}$. Finally, this implies that $RB = \frac{5}{2}x = \frac{125}{96}$, so our answer is $125 + 96 = 221$.

18

Alternate Solution: We will use analytic geometry. We set the coordinate plane such that B is at the origin, $A = (0, 3)$, and $C = (4, 0)$. First, let's find P:

We know that P is on the perpendicular bisector of $\overline{AB}$ given by the equation $y = \frac{3}{2}$, so $P = \left(p, \frac{3}{2}\right)$ for some real number p. Writing the equation $PB = PM$ we get $\sqrt{p^2 + \frac{9}{4}} = |2 - p|$. Solving this gives $p = \frac{7}{16}$, and hence $P = \left(\frac{7}{16}, \frac{3}{2}\right)$.

Then we similarly find Q:

Q is on the perpendicular bisector of $\overline{BC}$ which has the equation $x = 2$. So, $Q = (2, q)$ for some real number q. Writing $QB = QM$ gives $\sqrt{4 + q^2} = \left|q - \frac{3}{2}\right|$. Solving this we get $q = -\frac{7}{12}$, and $Q = \left(2, -\frac{7}{12}\right)$.

Now, since $\overline{PM}$ is horizontal and $\overline{QM}$ is vertical, $\angle PMQ = 90°$. Therefore, R is the midpoint of PQ. We find that $R = \left(\frac{39}{32}, \frac{11}{24}\right)$.

Finally,

$$BR = \sqrt{\left(\frac{39}{32}\right)^2 + \left(\frac{11}{24}\right)^2} = \frac{1}{96} \cdot \sqrt{117^2 + 44^2} = \frac{125}{96}.$$

The answer is $125 + 96 = 221$.

10. Let N be the number of nonempty subsets $S \subseteq \{1, 2, \ldots, 15\}$ such that S has no subsets of the form $\{n, 2n\}$ or $\{n, 2n + 1\}$ for any integer n. Find the remainder when N is divided by 1000.

Answer (305):

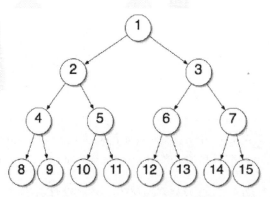

This is a binary tree with four levels. We do some casework on a subset S.

If $1 \in S$, then S cannot have 2 or 3. This leaves us with four independent triples $\{4, 8, 9\}$, $\{5, 10, 11\}$, $\{6, 12, 13\}$, $\{7, 14, 15\}$. For each triple $\{n, 2n, 2n + 1\}$, there are 5 choices: Any of the 2^3 subsets except for $\{n, 2n\}$, $\{n, 2n + 1\}$, and $\{n, 2n, 2n + 1\}$. So, if $1 \in S$ we get $5^4 = 625$ cases.

If $1 \notin S$, then we have two independent branches with 2 and 3 at the roots. Consider the cases for the branch from 2. By the same logic as before, since there are two branches with the $\{n, 2n, 2n+1\}$ property, we get 5^2 cases. If we do, then we have $2^4 = 16$ since any subset of $\{8, 9, 10, 11\}$ is valid. So for each of the two branches we have $5^2 + 16 = 41$ cases, leading to a total of $41^2 = 1681$ cases.

Summing up all the cases, we get $1681 + 625 - 1 = 2305$ (don't forget to subtract the empty set!). The answer is 305.

Alternate Solution: Let's divide the numbers into 4 groups as follows:

$$A = \{1\}, \ B = \{2, 3\}, \ C = \{4, 5, 6, 7\}, \ D = \{8, 9, 10, 11, 12, 13, 14, 15\}.$$

For each element we select from any of the first three groups, we won't be able to select exactly two elements from the next group.

Case 1: $1 \in S$. Then $2, 3 \notin S$. If we select k elements from C, then we cannot select $2k$ elements from D but we can select any subset of the remaining $8 - 2k$ terms. So, there are $\binom{4}{0} \cdot 2^8 + \binom{4}{1} \cdot 2^6 + \binom{4}{2} \cdot 2^4 + \binom{4}{3} \cdot 2^2 + \binom{4}{4} \cdot 2^0 = (1 + 4)^4 = 625$ subsets in this case.

Case 2: $1 \notin S$. This leads to three subcases based on 2 and 3 being in S or not:

Subcase 1: $2 \notin S$ and $3 \notin S$. With the same calculations as in *Case 1*, there are $625 - 1$ subsets here. Note that we are subtracting 1 because of the empty set.

Subcase 2: Either $2 \in S$ or $3 \in S$, but not both. Then we can select at most two elements from C. So, in this (sub)case the number of subsets is

$$2\left(\binom{2}{0} \cdot 2^8 + \binom{2}{1} \cdot 2^6 + \binom{2}{2} \cdot 2^4\right) = 2(256 + 128 + 16) = 800.$$

Subcase 3: $2 \in S$ and $3 \in S$. Then we cannot select any elements from C. So, in this (sub)case, the number of subsets is

$$2^8 = 256.$$

In total, there are $625 + 624 + 800 + 256 = 2305$ valid subsets, so the answer is 305.

11. The sequence $\{x_i\}$ satisfies $x_1 = \frac{1}{3}$ and $x_{n+1} = x_n^2 + x_n$ for all $n \geq 1$. Determine the value of

$$\left\lfloor \frac{x_1}{1 + x_1} + \frac{x_2}{1 + x_2} + \frac{x_3}{1 + x_3} + \cdots + \frac{x_{1000}}{1 + x_{1000}} \right\rfloor.$$

For a real number x, $\lfloor x \rfloor$ denotes the largest integer less than or equal to x.

Answer (997): Let $S = \frac{x_1}{1+x_1} + \frac{x_2}{1+x_2} + \frac{x_3}{1+x_3} + \cdots + \frac{x_{1000}}{1+x_{1000}}$. We have

$$S = 1000 - \left(\frac{1}{1+x_1} + \frac{1}{1+x_2} + \frac{1}{1+x_3} + \cdots + \frac{1}{1+x_{1000}} \right).$$

To write this as a telescopic sum, we play with the term $\frac{1}{1+x_n}$ using the recursion identity:

$$\frac{1}{1+x_n} = \frac{x_n}{x_n + x_n^2} = \frac{x_n}{x_{n+1}} = \frac{x_n^2}{x_n x_{n+1}} = \frac{x_{n+1} - x_n}{x_n x_{n+1}} = \frac{1}{x_n} - \frac{1}{x_{n+1}}.$$

Then, S becomes

$$1000 - \left(\frac{1}{x_1} - \frac{1}{x_{1001}} \right) = 1000 - \left(3 - \frac{1}{x_{1001}} \right) = 997 + \frac{1}{x_{1001}}.$$

Finally, note that $\{x_n\}$ is an increasing sequence, so $x_n > x_1 = \frac{1}{3}$ for all n, and thus $x_{n+1} > x_n + \frac{1}{9}$. This implies that $x_7 > x_1 + 6 \cdot \frac{1}{9} = 1$ and $x_{1001} > x_7 = 1$. We conclude that the answer is

$$\left\lfloor 997 + \frac{1}{x_{1001}} \right\rfloor = 997.$$

12. Find the number of ways to color the squares of a 8×8 checkerboard with red and blue such that every 2×2 sub-square contains exactly two red squares. Rotations and reflections are considered distinct.

Answer (510): There are $2^8 = 256$ ways to color the top row. We will split these arrangements into two cases: those with no adjacent, same-colored pairs, and those with adjacent, same-colored pairs.

Case 1: If there are no adjacent, same-colored pairs in the top row, then the colors must alternate. Then, the criteria will be satisfied only if every row in the entire board also has alternating colors. For every row, there are two ways to choose the coloring, whether it starts with red or blue, for a total of $2^8 = 256$ ways.

Case 2: If there are adjacent, same-colored pairs in the top row, then the second row is uniquely determined. Starting from one of these same-colored pairs, the two squares below this pair must be the opposite color to satisfy the rule. Then, we can build left and right, coloring squares so that they satisfy the 2 by 2 square rule. Every row below this row will also be uniquely determined, using the same method. Therefore, there are a total of $2^8 - 2 = 254$ ways, since 2 of the top row arrangements do not have same-color adjacent pairs.

Hence, there are a total of $256 + 254 = 510$ pairs.

13. The numbers $1, 2, 3, \ldots, 100$ are written on a blackboard. Every second for 20 seconds, Carl selects three numbers a, b, c on the board such that $a + b + c$ is also on the board, erases all four numbers, and writes down $a + b$, $b + c$, and $c + a$ instead. After 20 seconds, the reciprocals of the numbers remaining on the board are the roots of the polynomial

$$x^{80} + a_{79}\, x^{79} + \ldots + a_2\, x^2 + a_1\, x + a_0.$$

What is the sum of all distinct prime factors of $\frac{a_2}{a_0}$?

Answer (271): Note that if the numbers left on the board are $r_1, r_2, \cdots, r_{80}$, then the given polynomial is

$$\left(x - \frac{1}{r_1}\right) \cdots \left(x - \frac{1}{r_{80}}\right) = \frac{(r_1 x - 1) \ldots (r_{80} x - 1)}{r_1 \ldots r_{80}}.$$

Focusing on x^2 and constant terms in the expansion on the right, we get

$$a_2 = \frac{1}{r_1 \cdots r_{80}} \sum_{j<k} r_j r_k \quad \text{and} \quad a_0 = \frac{1}{r_1 \cdots r_{80}}.$$

Hence,

$$\frac{a_2}{a_0} = \sum_{j<k} r_j r_k.$$

To find this sum the key observation is that both the sum and the sum of squares on the board remain invariant under the operation, because

$$a + b + c + (a + b + c) = (a + b) + (b + c) + (c + a)$$

as well as

$$a^2 + b^2 + c^2 + (a + b + c)^2 = (a + b)^2 + (b + c)^2 + (c + a)^2.$$

Hence, we have

$$\frac{a_2}{a_0} = \sum_{j<k} r_j r_k = \frac{(r_1 + \ldots + r_{80})^2 - (r_1^2 + \ldots + r_{80}^2)}{2}$$

$$= \frac{(1 + 2 + \cdots + 100)^2 - (1^2 + 2^2 + \ldots + 100^2)}{2}$$

$$= \frac{100^2 \cdot 101^2}{8} - \frac{100 \cdot 101 \cdot 201}{12}$$

$$= \frac{100 \cdot 101}{24} \cdot (3 \cdot 100 \cdot 101 - 2 \cdot 201)$$

$$= \frac{25 \cdot 101}{6} \cdot (3 \cdot 100^2 - 100 - 2)$$

$$= \frac{25 \cdot 101}{6} \cdot (100 - 1)(3.100 + 2)$$

$$= 25 \cdot 101 \cdot 33 \cdot 151$$

whose prime factorization is

$$3 \cdot 5^2 \cdot 11 \cdot 101 \cdot 151.$$

Therefore, the answer is $3 + 5 + 11 + 101 + 151 = 271$.

14. Acute triangle ABC has orthocenter H and side length $BC = 12$. Denote M and N as the midpoints of $\overline{BH}$ and $\overline{CH}$. If the circumcircle of $\triangle HMN$ is tangent to the circumcircle of $\triangle ABC$, and $\tan \angle BAC = 7$, then the area of $\triangle ABC$ can be expressed in the form $\frac{p}{q}$ where p and q are relatively prime positive integers. Find $p + q$.

Answer (115):

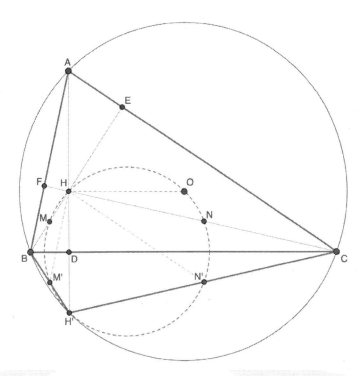

Let (XYZ) denote the circumcircle of $\triangle XYZ$. Let H' be the reflection of H over BC. As such, H' lies on (ABC), because $\angle HBC = \angle HAC = \angle H'BC$. Let M' and N' be the midpoints of BH' and CH'. Note that $(H'M'N')$ is tangent to (ABC) since the former is the image of the latter under a homothety of scale factor $\frac{1}{2}$ at H'.

Lemma: $(H'M'N')$ and (HMN) are the same circle.

Proof. Suppose otherwise; note that BC is the radical axis of $(H'M'N')$ and (HMN). Let T be the tangency point of (HMN) and (ABC) and let $\ell_{H'}$ and ℓ_T be the tangent lines to (ABC) at H' and T, respectively.

By the Radical Axis Theorem on $(H'M'N')$ and (HMN), we know that BC, $\ell_{H'}$, and ℓ_T concur. However, this is impossible unless $H' = T$ because H' and T are both on the same side of BC, and different tangent lines to (ABC) here intersect BC at different points. Thus, H' lies on (HMN).

(HMN) and $(H'M'N')$ are circles of the same size that are both inside (ABC) and tangent to (ABC) at the same point. Hence, they must be the same circle, finishing the proof of the Lemma.

By the Lemma, $HMNH'M'N'$ is cyclic. This circle is the image of (ABC) under a homothety centered at H' with scale factor $\frac{1}{2}$. The homothety maps A to H, so H is the midpoint of AH'.

Using the Law of Sines on $\triangle BAH$ and $\triangle ABC$, we get

$$\frac{AH}{\sin(90° - \angle A)} = \frac{AB}{\sin(\angle A + \angle B)} = \frac{AB}{\sin(\angle C)} = \frac{BC}{\sin(\angle A)}.$$

Thus,

$$AH = \frac{BC}{\tan(\angle A)} = \frac{12}{7}.$$

If D is the foot of the perpendicular from A to BC, note that

$$AD = AH + DH = \frac{3}{2}AH = \frac{18}{7}.$$

Therefore, the area of $\triangle ABC$ is

$$\frac{1}{2} \cdot BC \cdot AD = \frac{1}{2} \cdot 12 \cdot \frac{18}{7} = \frac{108}{7}$$

and the answer is $108 + 7 = 115$.

15. At Hilbert High School, 1000 lockers are arranged in a circle and numbered $1, 2, \ldots, 1000$ in that order. Each locker can be in one of three states: locked, unlocked (but closed) or open. Cindy begins by going around and playing with the lockers. When she visits a locker, she unlocks it if is locked, opens it if it is unlocked, and locks it if it is open. Initially all of them are locked. During her first trip, Cindy visits all the lockers starting with locker 1, unlocking them until she gets back to locker 1 (which is left unlocked but not opened yet). Then, Cindy visits lockers $1, 3, 5$, and so on, opening them until she returns to locker 1 (which is left open). Next, Cindy visits every third locker $1, 4, 7, \ldots, 997, 1000, 3, 6, 9, \ldots, 996, 999, 2, 5, \ldots, 998$ (in other words, every locker), locking each open locker and opening each unlocked one. Cindy continues this procedure, visiting every fourth locker, fifth locker, and so on, always starting and ending at locker 1. After her 1000th trip, how many lockers are locked?

Answer (370): Given $x \in \{1, 2, \ldots, 1000\}$, let us find the number of times locker x was visited. It is visited during K-th trip if and only if $x \equiv 1 + aK \pmod{1000}$ for some positive integer a. This is equivalent to $x - 1$ being divisible by $d = gcd(1000, K)$. Since d is a divisor of 1000 and $x - 1$, it also divides $gcd(1000, x - 1)$. For each divisor d of $gcd(1000, x - 1)$, we can count the number of K's such that $d = gcd(1000, K)$, but this is just $\varphi(1000/d)$, where φ is the Euler's totient function.

So, the number of visits of locker x is given by the following function of $g = gcd(1000, x - 1)$:

$$v(g) = \sum_{d \mid g} \varphi\left(\frac{1000}{d}\right).$$

We find the following φ values (mod 3) for divisors of 1000:

$\varphi(1) \equiv 1$	$\varphi(5) \equiv 1$	$\varphi(25) \equiv 2$	$\varphi(125) \equiv 1$
$\varphi(2) \equiv 1$	$\varphi(10) \equiv 1$	$\varphi(50) \equiv 2$	$\varphi(250) \equiv 1$
$\varphi(4) \equiv 2$	$\varphi(20) \equiv 2$	$\varphi(100) \equiv 1$	$\varphi(500) \equiv 2$
$\varphi(8) \equiv 1$	$\varphi(40) \equiv 1$	$\varphi(200) \equiv 2$	$\varphi(1000) \equiv 1$

The advantage of writing in this way is that all multiples of a certain number appear in a rectangular box with that number appearing in the upper left corner. Using this list we form the following table:

g	1	2	4	5	8	10	20	25	40	50	100	125	200	250	500	1000
$v(g)$ (mod 3)	1	0	1	0	2	0	0	1	0	0	1	2	2	0	2	1

Finally, $v(g)$ is a multiple of 3 for $g = 2, 5, 10, 20, 40, 50$, and 250. For a given g dividing 1000, the number of x values in $\{1, 2, \ldots, 1000\}$ such that $g = gcd(1000, x-1)$ is $\varphi(1000/g)$. So, the number of x such that locker x is locked at the end of Cindy's game is

$$
\begin{aligned}
& \varphi(500) + \varphi(200) + \varphi(100) + \varphi(50) + \varphi(25) + \varphi(20) + \varphi(4) \\
=\ & 200 + 80 + 40 + 20 + 20 + 8 + 2 \\
=\ & 370.
\end{aligned}
$$

AIME PRACTICE TESTS VOL 1

TEST-2

INSTRUCTIONS

1. This test has 15 questions. All answers are integers ranging from 0 to 999, inclusive. Your score will be the number of correct answers; i.e., there is neither partial credit nor a penalty for wrong answers.

2. No aids other than scratch paper, graph paper, ruler, compass, and protractor are permitted. In particular, calculators are **not** permitted.

3. Figures are not necessarily drawn to scale.

4. You will have **3 hours** to complete the test.

1. There are five boys and five girls in a math club. A subset of at least two students is chosen to participate in a math competition. Given that each subset is equally likely to be chosen, the probability that the selected team contains at least one boy and at least one girl can be expressed as $\frac{m}{n}$, where m and n are relatively prime positive integers. Find m.

2. Let ABC be a triangle with $AB = 21$ and $AC = 29$. Point M is the midpoint of BC, and $AM = 10$. Find the area of $\triangle ABC$.

3. Let a and b be two positive integers larger than 1 such that

$$\frac{\log_b a}{\log_a b}$$

is an integer with exactly 25 positive integer factors. Find the smallest possible number of digits in the base ten representation of ab.

4. A right circular cone C_1 is given with volume 20π. A dilation of positive ratio greater than 1 about the vertex of the cone sends C_1 to a cone C_2. A cube can be inscribed between C_2 and C_1 such that four of its vertices are on the circular portion of C_1. Let h be the minimum height of C_2 over all possible choices of C_1. If h can be written as $m\sqrt[3]{n}$ where m and n are positive integers and n is not divisible by any perfect cube larger than 1, find $m + n$.

5. A long contest lasts 42 days and contains 3 problems on each day. The possible scores for each problem are 0, 2, 5, or 7 points. Find the number of different possible total scores at the end of the contest.

6. Andrew writes the number n on a blackboard, where n is an integer between 1 and 1000, inclusive. At every step, if the number k is on the blackboard, he replaces it with $1000 - 2k$, continuing until he obtains a negative number, at which point he stops. Let $s(n)$ be the number of steps Andrew takes before he stops, given that he initially starts with n. For example, $s(400) = 3$ since Andrew stops after three steps: $400 \to 200 \to 600 \to -200$. Given that $s(n)$ is maximized when $n = N$, find the value of $N + s(N)$.

7. Let $S = \{(x, y) \mid x = 0, 1, \ldots, 8; \ y = 0, 1, \ldots, 8\}$, the set containing the 81 lattice points in the xy-plane with $0 \leq x, y \leq 8$. Let $\mathcal{R}$ denote the set of all rectangles whose four vertices belong to S and whose sides are parallel to the axes. The sum of the perimeters of all rectangles in $\mathcal{R}$ equals P. Find the remainder when P is divided by 1000.

8. Initially, the number 1 is written on a blackboard. Then, one of the digits 1, 2, 3, 4, 5 is appended at random to the end. This process continues until the resulting number in decimal notation is divisible by 25. Find the expected value of the number of the digits on the board when this occurs.

9. Let $\omega_1, \omega_2, \omega_3, \ldots, \omega_{21}$ be the distinct complex solutions of $x^{21} = 1$. Compute the value of

$$\sum_{k=1}^{200} \sum_{j=1}^{21} \omega_j^k.$$

10. Let $n = 3^a$ where a is a positive integer, and S be the set of positive integers $x < n$ such that $x^{\varphi(n)/2} - 1$ is not divisible by n, where $\varphi(n)$ is the number of positive integers less than n that are relatively prime to n. Find the smallest a such that $|S| \geq 4042$.

11. Let $a_1, a_2, \ldots, a_m$ be a strictly increasing sequence of m positive even integers. Similarly, let $b_1, b_2, \ldots, b_n$ be a strictly increasing sequence of n positive odd integers. Given that
$$a_1 + a_2 + \cdots + a_m + b_1 + b_2 + \cdots + b_n = 2025,$$
find the largest possible value of $3m + 4n$.

12. Given a unit cube, consider the six planes each containing a distinct face of the cube. Let $\mathcal{S}$ be the set of points in 3-dimensional space whose sum of distances to the given six planes is at most 12. Determine the volume of $\mathcal{S}$.

13. Four points are each randomly and uniformly selected on the circumference of a unit circle. The probability that the distances between the six pairs of these points are all less than 1 equals $\frac{a}{b}$, where a and b are relatively prime positive integers. Compute $a + b$.

14. A function f over the positive reals satisfies

$$f(x)f(yf(x)) = f(x+y)$$

for all $x, y \in (0, \infty)$. If $f(1) = \frac{1}{152}$ and $f(4) = \frac{p}{q}$ where p and q are relatively prime positive integers, compute $p + q$.

15. In triangle ABC, $\angle ABC$ is a right angle and the incircle ω is tangent to $\overline{BC}$, $\overline{CA}$, $\overline{AB}$ at D, E, F respectively. $\overline{AD}$ intersects ω again at P, and $\overline{PC} \perp \overline{PF}$. Given that $AC = 1000$, the length of AP equals $m\sqrt{n}$ where m and n are positive integers and n is not divisible by the square of any prime. Find $m + n$.

Test-2 Answer Key

1. 961

2. 210

3. 12

4. 33

5. 879

6. 343

7. 280

8. 26

9. 189

10. 8

11. 223

12. 271

13. 55

14. 606

15. 90

Test-2 Solutions

1. There are five boys and five girls in a math club. A subset of at least two students is chosen to participate in a math competition. Given that each subset is equally likely to be chosen, the probability that the selected team contains at least one boy and at least one girl can be expressed as $\frac{m}{n}$, where m and n are relatively prime positive integers. Find m.

   Answer (961): We will use complementary counting. The number of ways for the team to be all boys or all girls is

   $$2\left(\binom{5}{2} + \binom{5}{3} + \binom{5}{4} + \binom{5}{5}\right) = 52,$$

   and the total number of team selections is

   $$\binom{10}{2} + \binom{10}{3} + \binom{10}{4} + \cdots + \binom{10}{10} = 2^{10} - 10 - 1 = 1013.$$

   There are $1013 - 52 = 961$ desired selections, which gives a probability of $\frac{961}{1013}$. Since $961 = 31^2$ and 1013 (not a multiple of 31) are relatively prime, the answer is 961.

2. Let ABC be a triangle with $AB = 21$ and $AC = 29$. Point M is the midpoint of BC, and $AM = 10$. Find the area of $\triangle ABC$.

   Answer (210):

35

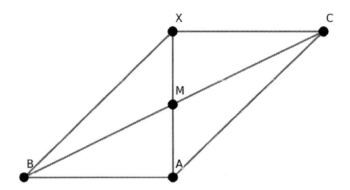

Motivated by the Pythagorean triple $(20, 21, 29)$, we suspect there is a convenient right triangle somewhere.

Indeed, if we reflect A over M to X, $ABXC$ is a parallelogram which implies $BX = AC = 29$, so ABX is a right triangle with side lengths 20, 21, and 29. Also, since $ABXC$ is a parallelogram, the areas of $\triangle ABC$ and $\triangle ABX$ are equal. Thus, the area of $\triangle ABC$ is $\frac{1}{2} \cdot 20 \cdot 21 = 210$.

Alternate Solution: Let $BM = MC = m$. Using Stewart's Theorem on $\triangle ABC$, we get

$$2 \cdot 10^2 m + 2m^3 = 21^2 m + 29^2 m.$$

Solving this, we find that $m = \sqrt{541}$. Observe that $m^2 = 10^2 + 21^2$, so $\triangle BAM$ is a right triangle with $\angle BAM = 90°$. Its area is then

$$\frac{1}{2} \cdot AB \cdot AM = \frac{1}{2} \cdot 10 \cdot 21 = 105$$

and the area of $\triangle ABC$ is twice this, which is 210.

3. Let a and b be two positive integers larger than 1 such that

$$\frac{\log_b a}{\log_a b}$$

is an integer with exactly 25 positive integer factors. Find the smallest possible number of digits in the base ten representation of ab.

Answer (12): Let $\log_b a = r$ for some real number r. Then note that $\log_a b = \frac{1}{\log_b a}$ and the given ratio is

$$\frac{\log_b a}{\log_a b} = (\log_b a)^2 = r^2.$$

It is given that $N = r^2$ is an integer with 25 factors. We would like to minimize $ab = b^{r+1}$. The smallest positive integer N with 25 factors is $2^4 \cdot 3^4 = 36^2$ and the smallest value of b is 2. This gives the solution $a = 2^{36}$ and $b = 2$. Thus, the smallest value of ab is 2^{37}.

To find the number of digits in 2^{37}, observe that

$$2^{30} \cdot 2^7 = (2^{10})^3 \cdot 2^7 > 10^9 \cdot 128.$$

So, 2^{37} has at least 12 digits. Since 2^{10} is very close to 1000, we expect it to have exactly 12 digits. One of many ways to show this is

$$2^{37} < 2^{39} = (2^{13})^3 < 10000^3 = 10^{12}.$$

We conclude that the answer is 12.

4. A right circular cone C_1 is given with volume 20π. A dilation of positive ratio greater than 1 about the vertex of the cone sends C_1 to a cone C_2. A cube can be inscribed between C_2 and C_1 such that four of its vertices are on the circular portion of C_1. Let h be the minimum height of C_2 over all possible choices of C_1. If h can be written as $m\sqrt[3]{n}$ where m and n are positive integers and n is not divisible by any perfect cube larger than 1, find $m + n$.

Answer (33): Let r_1 and h_1 be the radius and the height of C_1, respectively. Since the base circle of C_1 contains the top face of the cube, the cube has side lengths $r_1\sqrt{2}$. Then the height of C_2 is $h_1 + r_1\sqrt{2}$. Using the volume of C_1, we get $r_1^2 h_1 = 60$.

By the AM-GM inequality, we have

$$h_1 + r_1\sqrt{2} = h_1 + \frac{r_1}{\sqrt{2}} + \frac{r_1}{\sqrt{2}} \geq 3\sqrt[3]{\frac{h_1 r_1^2}{2}} = 3\sqrt[3]{30}.$$

This can be achieved when $r_1 = h_1\sqrt{2}$, or more precisely when $(r_1, h_1) = (2\sqrt[3]{30}, \sqrt[3]{30})$. Hence, $h = 3\sqrt[3]{30}$ is our desired minimum. The answer is $3 + 30 = 33$.

5. A long contest lasts 42 days and contains 3 problems on each day. The possible scores for each problem are 0, 2, 5, or 7 points. Find the number of different possible total scores at the end of the contest.

Answer (879): In total, there are 126 problems and a perfect score is 882. Call an integer in $[0, 882]$ *achievable* if it is a possible total score on the exam, and *unachievable* otherwise.

By performing the mapping $0 \leftrightarrow 7, 2 \leftrightarrow 5$, note that n is achievable if and only if $882 - n$ is achievable. Therefore, it suffices to find the number of unachievable numbers in the range $[0, 441)$, double it, and subtract the result from 883. (441 is achievable as 7×63.)

Let us first consider the range $[0, 10]$. Note that we can get even numbers up to 10 via 0's and 2's. For the odd numbers, 1 and 3 are unachievable, and the rest are achievable: $5 = 5$, $7 = 7$, and $9 = 2 + 7$.

Since the range $[4, 10]$ has 7 consecutive achievable numbers, all the integers in $[11, 441)$ are achievable by adding 7 to a smaller achievable number.

Therefore, there are only 2 unachievable numbers in the interval $[0, 441)$. By the note above, the answer is $883 - 2 \cdot 2 = 879$.

6. Andrew writes the number n on a blackboard, where n is an integer between 1 and 1000, inclusive. At every step, if the number k is on the blackboard, he replaces it with $1000 - 2k$, continuing until he obtains a negative number, at which point he stops. Let $s(n)$ be the number of steps Andrew takes before he stops, given that he initially starts with n. For example, $s(400) = 3$ since Andrew stops after three steps: $400 \to 200 \to 600 \to -200$. Given that $s(n)$ is maximized when $n = N$, find the value of $N + s(N)$.

Answer (343): Let $s(N) = m$ and $a_0, a_1, a_2, \ldots, a_m$ be the sequence defined by $a_0 = N$ and $a_k = 1000 - 2a_{k-1}$ for $1 \le k \le m$. We know that $a_0 = N \in [1, 1000]$, $a_1, a_2, \ldots, a_{m-1} > 0$, but $a_m < 0$.

To find the general form of this sequence, observe that $f(x) = 1000 - 2x$ has a fixed point at $x = \frac{1000}{3}$. Moreover, $f\left(\frac{1000}{3} + d\right) = \frac{1000}{3} - 2d$. So, letting $a_0 = \frac{1000}{3} + \Delta$ and applying f repeatedly k times will give us

$$a_0 = \frac{1000}{3} + \Delta \to \frac{1000}{3} - 2\Delta \to \frac{1000}{3} + 4\Delta \to \cdots \to a_k = \frac{1000}{3} + (-2)^k \Delta.$$

Observe that the terms of the sequence $\{a_k\}$ oscillate around the center $\frac{1000}{3}$ with the distance to the center doubling each time. To make the most number of terms positive, it is intuitive to start with the number that is closest to the center $\frac{1000}{3}$, i.e. $a_0 = 333$. This gives the following sequence reaching a negative number in $m = 10$ steps:

$$333 \to 334 \to 332 \to 336 \to 328 \to 344 \to 312 \to 376 \to 248 \to 504 \to -8.$$

Hence, the answer should be $333 + 10 = 343$.

We now formally prove that $m = 10$, and that $a_0 = 333$ is the only number leading to the maximum number of steps:

If $a_0 < 333$, then $a_0 = \frac{1000}{3} + \Delta \leq 332$, and so $\Delta \leq -\frac{4}{3}$. But then we see that $a_8 < 0$:

$$a_8 = \frac{1000}{3} + (-2)^8 \Delta \leq \frac{1000}{3} + 2^8 \cdot \frac{-4}{3} < 0.$$

If $a_0 > 333$, then $a_0 = \frac{1000}{3} + \Delta \geq 334$, and so $\Delta \geq \frac{2}{3}$. But then we see that $a_9 < 0$:

$$a_9 = \frac{1000}{3} + (-2)^9 \Delta \leq \frac{1000}{3} - 2^9 \cdot \frac{2}{3} < 0.$$

So, the only starting number giving a sequence of at least 10 positive integers is $a_0 = 333$.

Alternate Solution: We start with the same definitions as before: let $s(N) = m$ and $a_0, a_1, a_2, \ldots, a_m$ be the sequence defined by $a_0 = N$ and $a_k = 1000 - 2a_{k-1}$ for $1 \leq k \leq m$. We know that $a_0 = N \in [1, 1000]$, $a_1, a_2, \ldots, a_{m-1} > 0$, but $a_m < 0$.

The key observation is that for $1 \leq k \leq m - 1$,

$$a_k \in [A, B] \text{ for integers } A \leq B \implies a_{k-1} = \frac{1000 - a_k}{2} \in \left[\left\lceil \frac{1000 - B}{2} \right\rceil, \left\lfloor \frac{1000 - A}{2} \right\rfloor\right].$$

Note that the previous interval has length about $\frac{1000-A}{2} - \frac{1000-B}{2} = \frac{B-A}{2}$, which is half the length of the next interval. The plan is to start with a_{m-1} and go backwards, restricting a_k into smaller and smaller intervals as we continue until we get an interval containing a single integer.

First, we find the range for a_{m-1}:

$$a_m \leq -1 \implies a_{m-1} = \frac{1000 - a_m}{2} > 500,$$

$$a_{m-1} = 1000 - 2a_{m-2} \leq 1000 - 2 \cdot 1 = 998.$$

Then,

$$a_{m-1} \in [501, 998]$$
$$\Rightarrow a_{m-2} \in [1, 249]$$
$$\Rightarrow a_{m-3} \in [376, 499]$$
$$\Rightarrow a_{m-4} \in [251, 312]$$
$$\Rightarrow a_{m-5} \in [344, 374]$$
$$\Rightarrow a_{m-6} \in [313, 328]$$
$$\Rightarrow a_{m-7} \in [336, 343]$$
$$\Rightarrow a_{m-8} \in [329, 332]$$
$$\Rightarrow a_{m-9} \in [334, 335]$$
$$\Rightarrow a_{m-10} \in [333, 333].$$

Note that $m \geq 10$ because $a_0 = 333$ leads to a valid sequence that stops after 10 steps:

$$333 \to 334 \to 332 \to 336 \to 328 \to 344 \to 312 \to 376 \to 248 \to 504 \to -8.$$

Since $m \geq 10$, we must have $a_{m-10} = 333$. But m cannot be larger than 10 because $a_{m-11} = \frac{1000 - a_{m-10}}{2} = \frac{1000 - 333}{2}$ would not be an integer. We conclude that $m = 10$, $N = 333$, and the answer is $333 + 10 = 343$.

7. Let $S = \{(x, y) \mid x = 0, 1, \ldots, 8; \ y = 0, 1, \ldots, 8\}$, the set containing the 81 lattice points in the xy-plane with $0 \leq x, y \leq 8$. Let $\mathcal{R}$ denote the set of all rectangles whose four vertices belong to S and whose sides are parallel to the axes. The sum of the perimeters of all rectangles in $\mathcal{R}$ equals P. Find the remainder when P is divided by 1000.

Answer (280): A rectangle on a grid is defined by its two horizontal sides and two vertical sides. The perimeter of the rectangle determined by the horizontal sides at $0 \leq i_1 < i_2 \leq 8$ and vertical sides at $0 \leq j_1 < j_2 \leq 8$ is $2(i_2 - i_1 + j_2 - j_1)$. Therefore,

$$P = \sum_{0 \leq i_1 < i_2 \leq 8} \ \sum_{0 \leq j_1 < j_2 \leq 8} 2(i_2 - i_1 + j_2 - j_1).$$

We then proceed to calculate P:

$$
\begin{aligned}
P &= \sum_{0 \le i_1 < i_2 \le 8} \sum_{0 \le j_1 < j_2 \le 8} 2(i_2 - i_1) + \sum_{0 \le i_1 < i_2 \le 8} \sum_{0 \le j_1 < j_2 \le 8} 2(j_2 - j_1) \\
&= 4 \cdot \left(\sum_{0 \le i_1 < i_2 \le 8} \sum_{0 \le j_1 < j_2 \le 8} (j_2 - j_1) \right) \cdot \\
&= 4 \cdot \binom{9}{2} \sum_{0 \le j_1 < j_2 \le 8} (j_2 - j_1) \\
&= 4 \cdot \binom{9}{2} (8 \cdot 1 + 7 \cdot 2 + \cdots + 1 \cdot 8) \\
&= 4 \cdot 36 \cdot 2 \cdot (8 \cdot 1 + 7 \cdot 2 + 6 \cdot 3 + 5 \cdot 4) \\
&= 4 \cdot 36 \cdot 2 \cdot 60 = 17280.
\end{aligned}
$$

The answer is 280.

8. Initially, the number 1 is written on a blackboard. Then, one of the digits 1, 2, 3, 4, 5 is appended at random to the end. This process continues until the resulting number in decimal notation is divisible by 25. Find the expected value of the number of the digits on the board when this occurs.

Answer (26): We can only use the digits 1, 2, 3, 4, 5, so the only way to get a multiple of 25 is at some point to append a 2 immediately followed by a 5.

Let x be the expected number of digits we will add until we get a multiple of 25 if our starting number is not 2, and let y be the expected number of digits we will add until we get a multiple of 25 if our starting number is 2. Note that the problem is asking for $x + 1$ since we expect to add x more digits after the first digit on the board, which is 1 (not 2).

Considering the possibilities for the current and next digits being a 2 or not, we derive the following two equations:

$$
x = \frac{4}{5}(x + 1) + \frac{1}{5}(y + 1)
$$
$$
y = \frac{1}{5} \cdot 1 + \frac{3}{5}(x + 1) + \frac{1}{5}(y + 1).
$$

Solving this system, we find that $x = 25$ and $y = 20$. Hence, the answer is $x + 1 = 26$.

9. Let $\omega_1, \omega_2, \omega_3, \ldots, \omega_{21}$ be the distinct complex solutions of $x^{21} = 1$. Compute the value of

$$\sum_{k-1}^{200} \sum_{j-1}^{21} \omega_j^k.$$

Answer (189): Note that ω_j are the 21st roots of unity and can be written in the form $\omega_j = e^{i\frac{2\pi j}{21}}$, so $\sum_{j=1}^{21} \omega_j = 0$. More generally, we show the following:

Lemma: Given an integer k, we have

$$\sum_{j=1}^{21} \omega_j^k = \begin{cases} 0 & k \not\equiv 0 \pmod{21} \\ 21 & k \equiv 0 \pmod{21}. \end{cases}$$

Proof. The second case (where $k \equiv 0 \pmod{21}$) is obvious, since if k is a multiple of 21, then $\omega_j^k = 1$. For the first case, note that if $\gcd(k, 21) = 1$, then the ω_j^k terms are simply a permutation of the 21th roots of unity, and their sum is zero. Similarly, if $\gcd(k, 21) = 3$ or $\gcd(k, 21) = 7$, the ω_j^k terms collapse to a sum of 7th roots of unity or 3rd roots of unity added three and seven times, respectively. $\square$

The only nonzero terms in the outer sum occur when k is a multiple of 21. Hence, we have

$$\sum_{k=1}^{200} \sum_{j=1}^{21} \omega_j^k = \sum_{21 \mid k} 21 = 9 \times 21 = 189,$$

since there are nine multiples of 21 between 1 and 200, inclusive.

Remark: The lemma is a special case of the following theorem regarding roots of unity, which can be proven similarly:

Theorem: For any positive integer n, let $\omega_1, \omega_2, \ldots, \omega_n$ be the n roots of $x^n = 1$. Then for any integer k:

$$\sum_{j=1}^{n} \omega_j^k = \begin{cases} 0 & k \not\equiv 0 \pmod{n} \\ n & k \equiv 0 \pmod{n}. \end{cases}$$

10. Let $n = 3^a$ where a is a positive integer, and S be the set of positive integers $x < n$ such that $x^{\varphi(n)/2} - 1$ is not divisible by n, where $\varphi(n)$ is the number of positive integers less than n that are relatively prime to n. Find the smallest a such that $|S| \geq 4042$.

Answer (8): Let $1 \leq x < n$. We will count the number of elements in S doing casework based on x being a multiple of 3 or not:

• *Case 1: x is a multiple of 3.*

In this case, $x \in S$ because $x^{\varphi(n)/2} - 1$ is 1 less than a multiple of 3, so it cannot be a multiple of $n = 3^a$. This gives us $3^{a-1} - 1$ values of x in S.

• *Case 2: x is not a multiple of 3.*

Since $n = 3^a$ is a power of an odd prime, there exists a primitive root g mod n, i.e. $\{g, g^2, \ldots, g^{\varphi(n)}\}$ are all different mod n and they cover all the residues mod n that are relatively prime to n.

Since x is relatively prime to $n = 3^a$, we have $x \equiv g^i \pmod{n}$ for some $i \in [1, \varphi(n)]$. Then

$$x^{\varphi(n)/2} \equiv g^{i\varphi(n)/2}.$$

This is only congruent to 1 modulo n when i is even, because for odd i,

$$g^{i\varphi(n)/2} \equiv g^{\varphi(n)/2} \not\equiv g^{\varphi(n)} \equiv 1.$$

So, for x to be in S, we need i to be odd. There are 3^{a-1} odd i values in the range 1 to $\varphi(n) = 2 \cdot 3^{a-1}$. So, this case gives an additional 3^{a-1} numbers in S.

In total, there are $2 \cdot 3^{a-1} - 1$ elements in S.

We want the smallest a such that $2 \cdot 3^{a-1} - 1 \geq 4042$, which is 8.

Alternate Solution: We claim that S consists of values $1 \leq x < n$ such that $x \equiv 0$ or $2 \pmod 3$.

If $x \equiv 0 \pmod 3$, then $x^{3^{a-1}} - 1 \equiv 2 \pmod 3$ is not a multiple of 3, hence $x \in S$.

If $x \equiv 2 \pmod 3$, then $x^{3^{a-1}} - 1 \equiv 1 \pmod 3$ is similarly not a multiple of 3, hence $x \in S$.

Finally, if $x \equiv 1 \pmod 3$, by the Lifting the Exponent Lemma, we have

$$v_3(x^{3^{a-1}} - 1) = v_3(x - 1) + a - 1,$$

where $v_3(m)$ denotes the power of 3 in the prime factorization of positive integer m.

But, $v_3(x - 1) \geq 1$ because $3 \mid x - 1$. So, we have $v_3(x^{3^{a-1}} - 1) \geq a$ which means that $x^{3^{a-1}} \equiv 1 \pmod{3^a}$, and hence, $x \notin S$.

There are $2 \cdot 3^{a-1} - 1$ values of $1 \leq x < 3^a$ that are 0 or 2 (mod 3). Hence, as before, we find that the smallest a satisfying $2 \cdot 3^{a-1} - 1 \geq 4042$ is 8.

11. Let $a_1, a_2, \ldots, a_m$ be a strictly increasing sequence of m positive even integers. Similarly, let $b_1, b_2, \ldots, b_n$ be a strictly increasing sequence of n positive odd integers. Given that

$$a_1 + a_2 + \cdots + a_m + b_1 + b_2 + \cdots + b_n = 2025,$$

find the largest possible value of $3m + 4n$.

Answer (223): First, observe that

$$a_1 + a_2 + \cdots + a_m \geq 2 + 4 + \ldots + 2m = m(m+1)$$

and

$$b_1 + b_2 + \cdots + b_n \geq 1 + 3 + \ldots + 2n - 1 = n^2.$$

Therefore, $m^2 + m + n^2 \leq 2025$, so $\left(m + \frac{1}{2}\right)^2 + n^2 \leq \frac{8101}{4}$.

Then, using the Cauchy-Schwarz inequality, we get

$$3\left(m + \frac{1}{2}\right) + 4n \leq 5\sqrt{\left(m + \frac{1}{2}\right)^2 + n^2} \leq 5\sqrt{\frac{8101}{4}}.$$

This implies that

$$3m + 4n \leq \left\lfloor 5\sqrt{\frac{8101}{4}} - \frac{3}{2} \right\rfloor = 223.$$

We need to show that $3m + 4n$ can actually take on the value of 223. To get closer to the equality case in the Cauchy–Schwarz inequality, we want $m : n \approx 3 : 4$. Let $m = 3k + m_1$ and $n = 4k + n_1$ for some positive integer k, and integers n_1 and m_1 close to 0.

$$223 = 3(3k + m_1) + 4(4k + n_1) = 25k + 3m_1 + 4n_1.$$

If we take $k = 9$, then $-2 = 3m_1 + 4n_1$. The solution with m_1, n_1 closest to 0 is $m_1 = -2$, $n =_1= 1$. This gives $m = 25$, $n = 37$. Then $m^2 + m + n^2 = 2019 < 2025$; therefore, it works. For instance, the following sequences satisfy the conditions:

$$(a_1, a_2, \ldots a_{25}) = (2, 4, \ldots 50) \text{ and } (b_1,\ b_2,\ \ldots b_{35}, b_{36}, b_{37}) = (1, 3, \ldots 69, 71, 79).$$

Thus, 223 is achievable, and it is our answer.

12. Given a unit cube, consider the six planes each containing a distinct face of the cube. Let S be the set of points in 3-dimensional space whose sum of distances to the given six planes is at most 12. Determine the volume of S.

Answer (271): We will use analytic geometry. Place the cube so that the center is at the origin and the edges are parallel to the axes.

Let $P(x_1, y_1, z_1)$ be a point in space. The distances from P to the planes containing the top and bottom faces of the cube ($x = \frac{1}{2}$ and $x = -\frac{1}{2}$ planes) are $\left| x_1 - \frac{1}{2} \right|$ and $\left| x_1 + \frac{1}{2} \right|$, respectively. Considering similar distances to the other four planes, the sum of the distances from P to the six planes is given by

$$f(x_1) + f(y_1) + f(z_1), \text{ where } f(a) = \left| a + \frac{1}{2} \right| + \left| a - \frac{1}{2} \right|.$$

We will split S into four parts based on how many of x_1, y_1, and z_1 lie within the interval $I = \left[-\frac{1}{2}, \frac{1}{2} \right]$.

Case 1: x_1, y_1 and z_1 all lie in I.

Note that this region is the original unit cube, and because $f(x_1) + f(y_1) + f(z_1) = 1 + 1 + 1 \leq 12$, the entire unit cube (with volume 1) is part of S.

Case 2: Exactly two among x_1, y_1 and z_1 lie in I.

Note that there are 6 symmetrical cases here, because there are 3 ways to choose which of the three coordinates lie outside I and 2 ways to choose its sign. Without loss of generality, let $x_1 > \frac{1}{2}$ and y_1, z_1 be in I.

Then $f(x_1) + f(y_1) + f(z_1) = 2x_1 + 1 + 1 \leq 12$ simplifies to $x_1 \leq 5$. This gives the region:

$$\left\{ (x_1, y_1, z_1) \mid \frac{1}{2} < x_1 \leq 5, \ -\frac{1}{2} \leq y_1, z_1 \leq \frac{1}{2} \right\}.$$

This is a rectangular prism with dimensions $\frac{9}{2} \times 1 \times 1$, and has volume $\frac{9}{2}$. So, this case leads to a total volume of $6 \cdot \frac{9}{2} = 27$.

Case 3: Exactly one among x_1, y_1 and z_1 lies in I.

Note that this time, there are 12 symmetrical cases, because there are 3 ways to choose which of the three coordinates lies in I and 2^2 ways to choose the sign of the other two coordinates. Without loss of generality, let $x_1, y_1 > \frac{1}{2}$, and z_1 be in I.

Then $f(x_1) + f(y_1) + f(z_1) = 2x_1 + 2y_1 + 1 \leq 12$ simplifies to $x_1 + y_1 \leq \frac{11}{2}$. This gives the region:

$$\left\{ (x_1, y_1, z_1) \mid \frac{1}{2} < x_1, \ \frac{1}{2} < y_1, \ x_1 + y_1 \leq \frac{11}{2}, \ -\frac{1}{2} \leq z_1 \leq \frac{1}{2} \right\}.$$

This is a triangular prism with base on xy-plane with area $\frac{1}{2}(\frac{9}{2})^2$ and height 1. Its volume is $\frac{81}{8}$. So, this case leads to a total volume of $12 \cdot \frac{81}{8} = \frac{243}{2}$.

Case 4: None of the three numbers x_1, y_1 and z_1 lies in I.

There are $2^3 = 8$ symmetrical cases here, because there are 2 ways to choose the sign of each coordinate. Without loss of generality, let $x_1, y_1, z_1 > \frac{1}{2}$.

Then $f(x_1) + f(y_1) + f(z_1) = 2x_1 + 2y_1 + 2z_1 \leq 12$, or $x_1 + y_1 + z_1 \leq 6$ gives the region:

$$\left\{ (x_1, y_1, z_1) \mid \frac{1}{2} < x_1, \ \frac{1}{2} < y_1, \ \frac{1}{2} < z_1, \ x_1 + y_1 + z_1 \leq 6 \right\}.$$

This is a triangular pyramid with base area $\frac{1}{2}(\frac{9}{2})^2$ and height $\frac{9}{2}$. Its volume is $\frac{243}{16}$. So, the total volume in this case is $8 \cdot \frac{243}{16} = \frac{243}{2}$.

Therefore, the total volume of S is

$$1 + 27 + \frac{243}{2} + \frac{243}{2} = 271.$$

13. Four points are each randomly and uniformly selected on the circumference of a unit circle. The probability that the distances between the six pairs of these points are all less than 1 equals $\frac{a}{b}$, where a and b are relatively prime positive integers. Compute $a+b$.

Answer (55): Note that the distance between two points on a unit circle is less than 1 if and only if the angle of the minor arc joining them is less than $60°$. Thus, we want all four points to lie on an arc of angle $60°$.

Let's mark these points using the colors red, green, blue and black. Define $P(\text{red})$ as the probability that green, blue, and black points all lie on the arc of angle $60°$, spanning clockwise starting at the red point. Similarly, define $P(\text{green})$, $P(\text{blue})$, and $P(\text{black})$.

We may assume that the four points are all different because the probability of two of the points coinciding is 0. Whenever the four points lie on an arc of angle $60°$, exactly one of them comes first going clockwise on the arc. Hence, the desired probability is the same as

$$P(\text{red}) + P(\text{green}) + P(\text{blue}) + P(\text{black}).$$

Finally, note that each term here is $\frac{1}{6^3}$ because there is $\frac{1}{6}$ chance for each of the remaining points to lie within the $60°$ arc starting at our point. Thus, the probability is $4 \cdot \frac{1}{6^3} = \frac{1}{54}$, and the answer is 55.

14. A function f over the positive reals satisfies

$$f(x)f(yf(x)) = f(x+y)$$

for all $x, y \in (0, \infty)$. If $f(1) = \frac{1}{152}$ and $f(4) = \frac{p}{q}$ where p and q are relatively prime positive integers, compute $p + q$.

Answer (606): Substituting $y = 1$ gives $f(f(x)) = \frac{f(x+1)}{f(x)}$. The similarity of the numerator and denominator after applying the function twice may suggest a function related to the reciprocal, potentially including an $x + 1$ expression as well. Indeed, the function $f(x) = \frac{1}{x+1}$ satisfies the functional equation requirement, though not the initial condition.

Adjusting coefficients for the initial condition, the function turns out to be $f(x) = \frac{1}{151x+1}$. Hence, $f(4) = \frac{1}{605}$, and the answer is 606.

With the following lemma, we will show that all the solutions to the functional equation must indeed be of the form $f(x) = \frac{1}{kx+1}$.

Lemma. Any function $f : (0, \infty) \to \mathbb{R}$ satisfying

$$f(x)f(yf(x)) = f(x+y), \ \forall x, y \in (0, \infty)$$

is either the constant 1 function or must be of the form $f(x) = \frac{1}{kx+1}$, for some positive constant k.

Proof. One common technique in functional equation problems is to choose the variables in a way to cancel some of the terms in the equation. We cannot make $x = x + y$ since $y > 0$. Trying $yf(x) = x + y$, we get $y = \frac{x}{f(x)-1}$. This would be in the domain of f (a positive number) only when $f(x) > 1$. So, assume that there is some x_0 with $f(x_0) > 1$. Then, if we plug in

$$x = x_0 \quad \text{and} \quad y = \frac{x_0}{f(x_0) - 1},$$

we obtain $f(x_0) = 1$, a contradiction. We conclude that $f(x) \leq 1$ for all $x > 0$.

Next, observe that since $f(yf(x)) \leq 1$, we have $f(x+y) \leq f(x)$. This shows that the function is monotone decreasing. It is, $b > a \Rightarrow f(b) \leq f(a)$.

We now claim that if $f(x_0) = 1$ for some $x_0 > 0$, then $f(x) = 1$ for all $x > 0$. When $x < x_0$, combining $f(x) \leq 1$ with $f(x) \geq f(x_0) = 1$, we reach $f(x) = 1$. Also, by substituting $x \to x_0$ in the functional equation, we get $f(y) = f(x_0 + y)$. Using this together with $f(x) = 1$ when $x \in (0, x_0]$, we conclude that $f(x) = 1$ for all $x > 0$.

So, if f is not the constant function 1, then $f(x) < 1$ everywhere. In this case, we see that f must be strictly decreasing, because $f(yf(x)) < 1$ and so $f(x + y) = f(x)f(yf(x)) < f(x)$. In particular, f is injective.

Using the given functional equation directly with the pairs $\left(x, \frac{y}{f(x)}\right)$ and $\left(y, \frac{x}{f(y)}\right)$, we obtain

$$f\left(x + \frac{y}{f(x)}\right) = f(x)f(y) = f\left(y + \frac{x}{f(y)}\right).$$

By injectivity, we see that

$$x + \frac{y}{f(x)} = y + \frac{x}{f(y)} \implies \frac{\frac{1}{f(x)} - 1}{x} = \frac{\frac{1}{f(y)} - 1}{y}.$$

Thus, $\frac{\frac{1}{f(x)} - 1}{x} = k$ for some positive constant k, and $f(x) = \frac{1}{kx+1}$.

15. In triangle ABC, $\angle ABC$ is a right angle and the incircle ω is tangent to $\overline{BC}$, $\overline{CA}$, $\overline{AB}$ at D, E, F respectively. $\overline{AD}$ intersects ω again at P, and $\overline{PC} \perp \overline{PF}$. Given that $AC = 1000$, the length of AP equals $m\sqrt{n}$ where m and n are positive integers and n is not divisible by the square of any prime. Find $m + n$.

Answer (90):

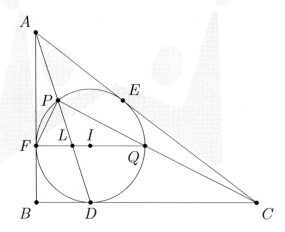

Let $BC = a$, $CA = b$, $AB = c$, and r be the inradius. We will use coordinate geometry. To simplify the equations, we scale the diagram so that $r = 1$. We will scale back at the end to find the actual values.

Orienting our coordinate plane so that $B = (0,0)$, $A = (0,c)$, and $C = (a,0)$, we get $F = (0,1)$ and $D = (1,0)$. Let $P = (x,y)$.

From P being on $\overline{AD}$, we get $y = c - cx$. Also, using the power of point P with respect to the incircle, we have $AP \cdot AD = AF^2$. Writing this in x, y and simplifying gives us $x^2 + (y - c)^2 = \frac{(c-1)^4}{c^2+1}$. Solving this for x and y using $y = c - cx$ we get

$$(x, y) = \left(\frac{(c-1)^2}{c^2+1}, \frac{2c^2}{c^2+1} \right).$$

Next, we use $\angle FPC = 90°$. The equation with the product of slopes being -1 reduces to $(y - 1)y + x(x - a) = 0$. Plugging in the x and y values we have found above and simplifying the expressions, we get the following equation in a and c:

$$ac = a + 3c - 1.$$

To find a second relation between a and c, we use $r = 1$:

$$r = s - b \Rightarrow b = a + c - 2 \Rightarrow (a + c - 2)^2 = a^2 + c^2.$$

This reduces to $ac = 2a + 2c - 2$. Combining the two equations gives us $a = c + 1$. Now substituting this in one of the two equations earlier and solving it, we get $c = 3$, $a = 4$, and $b = 5$. Then (in the scaled version of the diagram) AP is $\frac{AF^2}{AD} = \frac{4}{\sqrt{10}}$.

Since AC here is 5 but was originally 1000, this is a 1:200 scale. So, in the original diagram, we have $AP = 200 \cdot \frac{4}{\sqrt{10}} = 80\sqrt{10}$, and the answer is $80 + 10 = 90$.

Alternate Solution: Let I be the incenter, Q be the second intersection of $\overline{PC}$ with the incircle (other than P), and L be the intersection of the segments $\overline{AD}$ and $\overline{FI}$.

Since $\angle FPQ = \angle FPC = 90°$, FQ is a diameter of the incircle. So, F, L, I, Q are on the same line which is parallel to $\overline{BC}$.

Let $a = BC$, $b = CA$, $c = AB$, and r be the inradius. Also, let $x = AP$, $y = PL$, and $z = LD$. We will look for information regarding the ratios $x : y : z$.

First, using the power of A with respect to the incircle we have $AP \cdot AD = AF^2$, which implies that $\frac{AP}{AD} = \frac{AF^2}{AD^2} = \frac{(c-r)^2}{c^2+r^2}$, or

$$\frac{x}{x+y+z} = \frac{(c-r)^2}{c^2+r^2}. \tag{1}$$

Next, using $\overline{FL} \parallel \overline{BD}$ we get

$$\frac{z}{x+y+z} = \frac{BF}{BA} = \frac{r}{c}. \tag{2}$$

Finally, using $\overline{LQ} \parallel \overline{BD}$ we find $\frac{y}{y+z} = \frac{LQ}{DC} = \frac{LI+IQ}{DC}$. But, $\triangle LID \sim \triangle DBA$ which gives $LI = \frac{r^2}{c}$. Plugging this in above along with $IQ = r$ and $DC = a - r$, we get $\frac{y}{y+z} = \frac{r^2+cr}{ca-cr}$ which simplifies to

$$\frac{y}{z} = \frac{r^2 + cr}{ca - 2cr - r^2}. \tag{3}$$

Using (1) and (2), we get

$$\frac{y}{x+y+z} = 1 - \left(\frac{r}{c} + \frac{(c-r)^2}{c^2+r^2} \right) = \frac{r(c^2 - r^2)}{c(c^2 + r^2)}. \tag{4}$$

Note that multiplying (2) and (3) gives (4). So, we get

$$\frac{r}{c} \cdot \frac{r^2 + cr}{ca - 2cr - r^2} = \frac{r(c^2 - r^2)}{c(c^2 + r^2)},$$

which simplifies to

$$r^2 - r(a + 3c) + ac = 0.$$

Since $\angle B = 90°$, plugging in $r = \frac{a+c-b}{2}$ and using $b^2 = a^2 + c^2$, we derive

$$a = 2b - 2c.$$

This with $4a^2 = 4b^2 - 4c^2$ gives us (by dividing the two equations) $4a = 2b + 2c$, and hence

$$c : a : b = 3 : 4 : 5.$$

Since $b = 1000$, we find that $c = 600$, $a = 800$, and $r = 200$. Finally, from (1) we get

$$AP = \frac{4}{10} \cdot AD = \frac{2}{5} \cdot 200\sqrt{10} = 80\sqrt{10},$$

and the answer is $80 + 10 = 90$.

AIME PRACTICE TESTS VOL 1

TEST-3

INSTRUCTIONS

1. This test has 15 questions. All answers are integers ranging from 0 to 999, inclusive. Your score will be the number of correct answers; i.e., there is neither partial credit nor a penalty for wrong answers.

2. No aids other than scratch paper, graph paper, ruler, compass, and protractor are permitted. In particular, calculators are **not** permitted.

3. Figures are not necessarily drawn to scale.

4. You will have **3 hours** to complete the test.

52

1. Bob the ant starts at "0" on a number line. Every second, he flips a fair coin and jumps 2 units in the positive direction if the coin lands heads or 5 units in the positive direction if the coin lands tails. He stops moving once he lands on a number greater than 10. The probability that Bob stops at an even number is $\frac{m}{n}$, where m and n are relatively prime positive integers. Find $m \mid n$.

2. Let S be the sum of all 4-digit integers $\overline{abcd}$ with distinct digits such that a, b, c form an arithmetic sequence and b, c, d form a geometric sequence. Find the remainder when S is divided by 1000.

3. Let N denote the number of ordered lists of seven (possibly empty) sets $(S_1, \ldots, S_7)$ for which
$$S_1 \subseteq S_2 \subseteq \cdots \subseteq S_7 \subseteq \{1, 2, \ldots, 7\}.$$
Find the remainder when N is divided by 1000.

4. Find the number of ordered triples of positive integers (a, b, c) satisfying $1 \le a, b, c \le 22$ such that for $f(x) = ax^2 + bx + c$, the sum $f(n-1) + f(n+1)$ is divisible by 3 for all integers n.

5. Let m be the minimum positive value of
$$S = \sum_{1 \le i < j \le 2021} a_i a_j,$$
where $a_1, a_2, \ldots, a_{2021} \in \{-1, 1\}$. Among the 2021 terms $a_1, a_2, \ldots, a_{2021}$, determine the least possible number of terms that can equal 1 such that $S = m$.

6. Let S be the sum of the absolute values of all real solutions x to the following equation:
$$\log_2 \left(\log_2 \left(\log_2 (x + 27) + 27 \right) + 27 \right) = x.$$
What are the last three digits of $\lfloor 2^{27} S \rfloor$?
For a real number r, $\lfloor r \rfloor$ denotes the largest integer not exceeding r.

7. Richard drops a large bouncy ball off of a balcony 150 feet above ground. The ball is made up of rubber and plastic such that it is twice as likely to bounce with rubber on the bottom than with plastic. If the ball reaches $\frac{3}{4}$ of its previous height when bouncing off rubber and $\frac{1}{4}$ of its previous height when bouncing off plastic, find the expected value for the total distance the ball travels, in feet, before coming to a rest.

8. Let $ABCD$ be a quadrilateral inscribed in a circle with diameter 1, where $\overline{AC}$ bisects the angle $\angle BAD$. It is given that $AC = \frac{7}{10}$ and $BD = \frac{3}{5}$. If the area of $ABCD$ is x, find the value of $1000x$.

9. Nine distinct non-zero integers $a, b, c, d, e, f, g, h,$ and i are placed into a 3×3 grid as shown:

a	b	c
d	e	f
g	h	i

For each row and column, the value of the third number added to the product of the first two numbers is the same. That is,

$$ab + c = de + f = gh + i = ad + g = be + h = cf + i.$$

Find the minimum possible sum of the absolute values of the nine integers.

10. Circle ω_1 has a diameter $\overline{AB}$ of length 81. Circle ω_2 has radius 36 and center A. Let C and D be the intersection points of the two circles, and let E be the intersection of ω_2 and segment $\overline{AB}$. Segment $\overline{CD}$ meets line AB at P. Point Q is on ω_2, and line QE intersects the circumcircle of $\triangle QPB$ again at point R. If $QP = 40$, the length of $\overline{BR}$ can be written as $a\sqrt{b}$ for positive integers a and b, where b is not divisible by the square of any prime number. Find $a + b$.

11. Cubic polynomial $P(x) = x^3 - cx - 1$ has roots $r, s,$ and t, where c is a positive real constant. Given
$$\frac{1}{r^2 + cr} + \frac{1}{s^2 + cs} + \frac{1}{t^2 + ct} = -2,$$
the sum of all possible values of c can be written in the form $\frac{m + \sqrt{n}}{k}$, where m, n, and k are positive integers with m and k relatively prime. Find $m + n + k$.

12. Point P is chosen on side $\overline{AB}$ of square $ABCD$ with side length 8. Let I_1 be the incenter of triangle APD, and let I_2 be the center of the circle tangent to segments $BC, CD,$ and DP. Furthermore, it is given that $I_1 I_2 = \frac{7\sqrt{2}}{2}$.

The length of AP can be written in the form $\frac{a - b\sqrt{c}}{d}$, where positive integers a, b, d have a greatest common divisor of 1 and c is not divisible by the square of any prime number. Find $a + b + c + d$.

13. A set is said to be *odd-sized* if it contains an odd number of elements. Define the product of a set of numbers to be the product of all its elements. For a set S, let $f(S)$ be the sum of the products of all odd-sized subsets of S. Let N be the sum of $f(T)$ as T ranges over all odd-sized subsets of $\{1, 2, 3, 4, 5, 6, 7\}$. Find the remainder when N is divided by 1000.

14. Let S be the sum of the squares of the areas of all noncongruent and nondegenerate triangles with integer side lengths and perimeter 30. Find the remainder when S is divided by 1000.

15. In triangle ABC, circles ω_1 and ω_2 with radii $9\sqrt{3}$ and $3\sqrt{3}$, respectively, are both tangent to each other and side $\overline{BC}$. Moreover, ω_1 is tangent to side $\overline{AB}$ and ω_2 is tangent to side $\overline{AC}$. The common external tangent line $\ell \neq BC$ to both circles intersects line AC at point E and line AB at point F. Given that $EC = 7$ and $FB = 57$, compute the minimum possible value of AF.

Test-3 Answer Key

1. 101

2. 890

3. 152

4. 343

5. 988

6. 294

7. 570

8. 147

9. 55

10. 23

11. 10

12. 79

13. 880

14. 85

15. 19

Test-3 Solutions

1. Bob the ant starts at "0" on a number line. Every second, he flips a fair coin and jumps 2 units in the positive direction if the coin lands heads or 5 units in the positive direction if the coin lands tails. He stops moving once he lands on a number greater than 10. The probability that Bob stops at an even number is $\frac{m}{n}$, where m and n are relatively prime positive integers. Find $m + n$.

   Answer (101): Bob moves at most 5 steps every second and stops as soon as he lands on a number that is larger than 10. So, he must end at either $11, 12, 13, 14,$ or 15. The even numbers he can end at are 12 and 14.

   The paths ending at 12 are $2 + 2 + 2 + 2 + 2 + 2$ and the three orderings of $5 + 5 + 2$. This gives a probability of
   $$\frac{1}{2^6} + 3 \cdot \frac{1}{2^3} = \frac{25}{64}.$$

   The paths ending at 14 are orderings of $2 + 2 + 5 + 5$ where the last term is a 5; otherwise, the path would have ended before 14. The probability in this case is
   $$3 \cdot \frac{1}{2^4} = \frac{3}{16}.$$

   Hence, the probability of Bob ending at an even number is
   $$\frac{25}{64} + \frac{3}{16} = \frac{37}{64},$$

   and the answer is $37 + 64 = 101$.

2. Let S be the sum of all 4-digit integers $\overline{abcd}$ with distinct digits such that a, b, c form an arithmetic sequence and b, c, d form a geometric sequence. Find the remainder when S is divided by 1000.

   Answer (890): Since b, c, d form a geometric sequence, we have $c^2 = b \cdot d$. By

59

first choosing c and then looking at different ways of factoring c^2, we get the following candidates for (b, c, d):

$$(1, 2, 4), (1, 3, 9), (2, 4, 8), (4, 6, 9)$$

and the reverse of these. Only the triples $(4, 2, 1)$ and $(4, 6, 9)$ lead to such 4-digit numbers which are 6421 and 2469. Thus, $S = 6421 + 2469 = 8890$, and the answer is 890.

3. Let N denote the number of ordered lists of seven (possibly empty) sets $(S_1, \ldots, S_7)$ for which
$$S_1 \subseteq S_2 \subseteq \cdots \subseteq S_7 \subseteq \{1, 2, \ldots, 7\}.$$
Find the remainder when N is divided by 1000.

Answer (152): Looking at any element of $\{1, 2, \ldots, 7\}$, we see that there are eight possibilities to assign the element: it can be in none of the S_i's, or it can be in $S_i, \ldots, S_7$ for some $i = 1, \ldots, 7$. Since these choices are independent from each other, we get

$$N = 8^7 = 2^{21} = 2^{10} \times 2^{11} \equiv 24 \times 48 \equiv 152 \pmod{1000}.$$

4. Find the number of ordered triples of positive integers (a, b, c) satisfying $1 \le a, b, c \le 22$ such that for $f(x) = ax^2 + bx + c$, the sum $f(n-1) + f(n+1)$ is divisible by 3 for all integers n.

Answer (343): We will show that a, b, c must all be multiples of 3.

Substituting $n = -1, 0, 1$ in $f(n-1) + f(n+1)$, we see that

$$3 \mid f(-2) + f(0), \quad 3 \mid f(-1) + f(1), \quad 3 \mid f(0) + f(2).$$

In terms of a, b, c, this means

$$3 \mid 4a - 2b + 2c, \quad 3 \mid 2a + 2c, \quad \text{and } 3 \mid 4a + 2b + 2c.$$

Adding these, we get $3 \mid 10a + 6c$ which implies $3 \mid a$. Next, $3 \mid 2a + 2c$ and $3 \mid a$, so $3 \mid c$. Finally, $3 \mid 4a + 2b + 2c$, $3 \mid a$ and $3 \mid c$, so $3 \mid b$.

There are 7 positive multiples of 3 under 22. This gives $7^3 = 343$ triples of (a, b, c).

They all work since they lead to functions f where $3 \mid f(n)$ for all integer n, and consequently $3 \mid f(n-1) + f(n+1)$.

5. Let m be the minimum positive value of

$$S = \sum_{1 \leq i < j \leq 2021} a_i a_j,$$

where $a_1, a_2, \ldots, a_{2021} \in \{-1, 1\}$. Among the 2021 terms $a_1, a_2, \ldots, a_{2021}$, determine the least possible number of terms that can equal 1 such that $S = m$.

Answer (988): Let $s = a_1 + a_2 + \ldots + a_{2021}$. Notice that

$$s^2 = (a_1^2 + a_2^2 + \ldots + a_{2021}^2) + 2S = 2021 + 2S.$$

So, in order to minimize S, we need to minimize $|s|$ while still keeping $|s| > \sqrt{2021}$ for S to be positive. Thus, $|s| = 45$. Checking $s = 45$ yields 1033 terms equal to 1 and $s = -45$ yields 988 terms equal to 1, so the smaller of the two, 988, is our answer.

6. Let S be the sum of the absolute values of all real solutions x to the following equation:

$$\log_2 \left(\log_2 \left(\log_2 (x + 27) + 27\right) + 27\right) = x.$$

What are the last three digits of $\lfloor 2^{2^7} S \rfloor$?
For a real number r, $\lfloor r \rfloor$ denotes the largest integer not exceeding r.

Answer (294): Let $f(x) = \log_2(x + 27)$, and let x be a root of $f(f(f(x))) = x$.

If $f(x) > x$, since f is increasing, taking f of both sides repeatedly, we get

$$x = f(f(f(x))) > f(f(x)) > f(x) > x,$$

a contradiction. After a similar contradiction for $f(x) < x$, we conclude that $f(x) = x$.

By investigating the graph of f, we find that $f(x) = x$ has two solutions, namely 5 and another root in $(-27, -26)$. Let's call this second root $x = -27 + \epsilon$. Then, we have $2^x = x + 27$ which implies $2^{-27+\epsilon} = \epsilon$. Since $0 < \epsilon < 1$, we get $2^{-27} < \epsilon < 2^{-26}$ or $1 < 2^{27} \epsilon < 2$.

Now, $S = 5 + (27 - \epsilon) = 32 - \epsilon$. So,

$$\lfloor 2^{27} S \rfloor = \lfloor 2^{27} \cdot 32 - 2^{27} \epsilon \rfloor = 2^{27} \cdot 32 - 2 = 2^{32} - 2.$$

This number modulo 1000 is

$$2^{30} \cdot 4 - 2 \equiv 24^3 \cdot 4 - 2 \equiv 3^3 \cdot 2^{11} - 2 \equiv 27 \cdot 48 - 2 \equiv 294.$$

62

7. Richard drops a large bouncy ball off of a balcony 150 feet above ground. The ball is made up of rubber and plastic such that it is twice as likely to bounce with rubber on the bottom than with plastic. If the ball reaches $\frac{3}{4}$ of its previous height when bouncing off rubber and $\frac{1}{4}$ of its previous height when bouncing off plastic, find the expected value for the total distance the ball travels, in feet, before coming to a rest.

Answer (570): Assume that if the ball drops off at a height of h feet, then it reaches a point that is H feet above the ground. The expected value of H is

$$h \cdot \left(P(\text{rubber}) \cdot \frac{3}{4} + P(\text{plastic}) \cdot \frac{1}{4} \right) = h \cdot \left(\frac{2}{3} \cdot \frac{3}{4} + \frac{1}{3} \cdot \frac{1}{4} \right) = \frac{7h}{12}.$$

Since each height is covered twice except the first one (a trip down and another one up), the expected value of the total distance is

$$2 \times 150 \left(1 + \frac{7}{12} + \frac{7^2}{12^2} + \ldots \right) - 150 = 2 \times 150 \times \frac{12}{5} - 150 = 570.$$

8. Let $ABCD$ be a quadrilateral inscribed in a circle with diameter 1, where $\overline{AC}$ bisects the angle $\angle BAD$. It is given that $AC = \frac{7}{10}$ and $BD = \frac{3}{5}$. If the area of $ABCD$ is x, find the value of $1000x$.

Answer (147): First observe that $BC = CD$ since $ABCD$ is cyclic and $\overline{AC}$ is an angle bisector. By Ptolemy's Theorem,

$$\frac{21}{50} = AC \cdot BD = AB \cdot CD + AD \cdot BC = AB \cdot BC + AD \cdot DC.$$

Now we know $\sin \angle B = \sin \angle D = \frac{AC}{1} = \frac{7}{10}$ by the Extended Law of Sines. Then the area of $ABCD$ is

$$\begin{aligned} x &= \frac{1}{2}(AB \cdot BC \sin \angle B + AD \cdot DC \sin \angle D) \\ &= \frac{1}{2}(AB \cdot BC + AD \cdot DC) \sin \angle B \\ &= \frac{1}{2} \cdot \frac{21}{50} \cdot \frac{7}{10} = \frac{147}{1000}. \end{aligned}$$

Hence, the answer is $1000x = 147$.

9. Nine distinct non-zero integers a, b, c, d, e, f, g, h, and i are placed into a 3×3 grid as shown:

a	b	c
d	e	f
g	h	i

For each row and column, the value of the third number added to the product of the first two numbers is the same. That is,

$$ab + c = de + f = gh + i = ad + g = be + h = cf + i.$$

Find the minimum possible sum of the absolute values of the nine integers.

Answer (55): Let $K = ab + c$ be the the constant sum.

From $cf + i = gh + i$ we get $cf = gh$. Substituting $c = K - ab$, $f = K - de$, $g = K - ad$, and $h = K - be$, we get

$$(K - ab)(K - de) = (K - ad)(K - be)$$

which reduces to

$$K(a - e)(b - d) = 0.$$

Since a, b, d, e are distinct numbers, this implies that $K = 0$. Then the grid turns into:

a	b	$-ab$
d	e	$-de$
$-ad$	$-be$	$-abde$

Note that $-1 \notin \{a, b, d, e\}$; otherwise, it would force two of the nine numbers to be the same.

We now perform casework on whether $1 \in \{a, b, d, e\}$:

- If $1 \in \{a, b, d, e\}$, then $p \in \{a, b, d, e\} \to -p \notin \{a, b, d, e\}$. Otherwise, since $\{a, b, d, e\}$ are in a 2×2 subgrid, p or $-p$ would be in the same row or column as 1 and the third number of that row or column would be $-p$ or p, contradicting the distinctness of the numbers. Thus, in this case, the minimum occurs when $\{|a|, |b|, |d|, |e|\} = \{1, 2, 3, 4\}$, and the desired sum is

$$34 + (|a| + |e|)(|b| + |d|) \leq 34 + 3 \cdot 7 = 55.$$

  The equality can be achieved, for instance, when $(a, b, d, e) = (1, 2, 3, 4)$.

- If $1 \notin \{a, b, d, e\}$, then at most two of $|a|, |b|, |d|, |e|$ can equal 2 and at most two can equal 3: Thus, we have

$$|a| + |b| + |d| + |e| + |ab| + |de| + |ad| + |be| + |abde|$$
$$= |a| + |b| + |d| + |e| + (|a| + |e|) \cdot (|b| + |d|) + |abde|$$
$$\geq (2 + 2 + 3 + 3) + (2 + 2)(3 + 3) + (2 \cdot 2 \cdot 3 \cdot 3) > 55.$$

We conclude that the answer is 55.

10. Circle ω_1 has a diameter $\overline{AB}$ of length 81. Circle ω_2 has radius 36 and center A. Let C and D be the intersection points of the two circles, and let E be the intersection of ω_2 and segment $\overline{AB}$. Segment $\overline{CD}$ meets line AB at P. Point Q is on ω_2, and line QE intersects the circumcircle of $\triangle QPB$ again at point R. If $QP = 40$, the length of $\overline{BR}$ can be written as $a\sqrt{b}$ for positive integers a and b, where b is not divisible by the square of any prime number. Find $a + b$.

Answer (23):

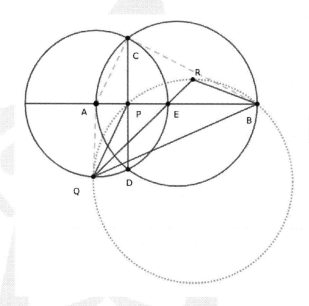

Note that since Q, P, R, and B are concyclic, $\triangle BRE \sim \triangle QPE$. Therefore, $\frac{BR}{BE} = \frac{QP}{QE}$. We are given that $QP = 40$. To find BR, it remains to find BE and QE.

First, $BE = BA - EA = 81 - 36 = 45$. To find QE, we look at the isosceles triangle $\triangle QAE$. If we let $\angle QAE = 2\theta$, then $QE = 2 \cdot QA \cdot \sin\theta = 72\sin\theta$.

We will use $\triangle QAP$ to find $\sin\theta$. It is given that $QP = 40$ and $QA = 36$.

To find AP, note that $\triangle APC \sim \triangle CPB$ because $\angle ACB = \angle APC = 90°$. So, we have $\frac{AP}{CA} = \frac{CA}{AB}$, which gives $AP = \frac{CA^2}{AB} = \frac{36^2}{81} = 16$.

Using the Law of Cosines on $\triangle QAP$, we get

$$AQ^2 + AP^2 - 2 \cdot AQ \cdot AP \cdot \cos(2\theta) = QP^2$$
$$\Rightarrow \quad 36^2 + 16^2 - 2 \cdot 36 \cdot 16 \cos(2\theta) = 40^2$$
$$\Rightarrow \quad \cos(2\theta) = -\frac{1}{24}.$$

Then from $\cos(2\theta) = 1 - 2\sin^2(\theta)$, we get $\sin\theta = \frac{5\sqrt{3}}{12}$.

Going back, we first find that $QE = 72\sin\theta = 30\sqrt{3}$. Finally,

$$\frac{BR}{BE} = \frac{QP}{QE} \Rightarrow BR = \frac{BE \cdot QP}{QE} = \frac{45 \cdot 40}{30\sqrt{3}} = 20\sqrt{3}.$$

Hence, the answer is $20 + 3 = 23$.

11. Cubic polynomial $P(x) = x^3 - cx - 1$ has roots r, s, and t, where c is a positive real constant. Given

$$\frac{1}{r^2 + cr} + \frac{1}{s^2 + cs} + \frac{1}{t^2 + ct} = -2,$$

the sum of all possible values of c can be written in the form $\frac{m+\sqrt{n}}{k}$, where m, n, and k are positive integers with m and k relatively prime. Find $m + n + k$.

Answer (10): For a function f, we will express $f(r) + f(s) + f(t)$ by the cyclic sum notation: $\sum\limits_{cyc} f(r)$.

To make the fraction easier to deal with, we break it up as follows:

$$\sum_{cyc} \frac{1}{r^2 + cr} = \sum_{cyc} \frac{1}{c}\left(\frac{1}{r} - \frac{1}{r+c}\right) = \frac{1}{c}\left(\sum_{cyc} \frac{1}{r} - \sum_{cyc} \frac{1}{r+c}\right).$$

First, we evaluate

$$\sum_{cyc} \frac{1}{r} = \frac{rs + st + rt}{rst} = \frac{-c}{1} = -c$$

using Vieta's formulas. Next, let $r' = r + c, s' = s + c$, and $t' = t + c$. We will then create a cubic polynomial with roots r', s', t'. We may write

$$P(x) = (x - r)(x - s)(x - t) \implies P(x - c) = (x - r')(x - s')(x - t'),$$

so our desired cubic is $P(x - c)$. Expanding, we see that

$$P(x - c) = (x - c)^3 - c(x - c) - 1 = x^3 - 3cx^2 + (3c^2 - c)x - (c^3 - c^2 + 1).$$

Using Vieta's formulas, we get $r's' + s't' + r't' = 3c^2 - c$ and $r's't' = c^3 - c^2 + 1$. Hence,

$$\sum_{cyc} \frac{1}{r+c} = \frac{1}{r'} + \frac{1}{s'} + \frac{1}{t'} = \frac{r's' + s't' + r't'}{r's't'} = \frac{c(3c-1)}{c^3 - c^2 + 1}.$$

So, it remains to solve

$$\frac{1}{c}\left(-c - \frac{c(3c-1)}{c^3 - c^2 + 1}\right) = -2 \implies -1 - \frac{3c-1}{c^3 - c^2 + 1} = -2,$$

which upon further rearrangement translates to $3c - 1 = c^3 - c^2 + 1$ or $c^3 - c^2 - 3c + 2 = 0$. A quick check shows that $c = 2$ is a solution, so $(c-2)(c^2 + c - 1) = 0$.

To finish, we see that the quadratic $c^2 + c - 1$ has two solutions: $\frac{-1 \pm \sqrt{5}}{2}$. Adding the positive solution $\frac{-1+\sqrt{5}}{2}$ to 2 yields a sum of $\frac{3+\sqrt{5}}{2}$, so our final answer is $3 + 5 + 2 = 10$.

12. Point P is chosen on side $\overline{AB}$ of square $ABCD$ with side length 8. Let I_1 be the incenter of triangle APD, and let I_2 be the center of the circle tangent to segments BC, CD, and DP. Furthermore, it is given that $I_1 I_2 = \frac{7\sqrt{2}}{2}$.

The length of AP can be written in the form $\frac{a - b\sqrt{c}}{d}$, where positive integers a, b, d have a greatest common divisor of 1 and c is not divisible by the square of any prime number. Find $a + b + c + d$.

Answer (79):

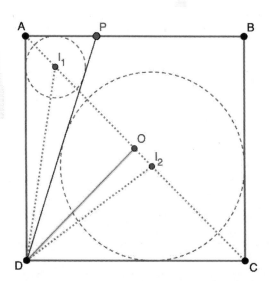

Let $\theta = \angle ADI_1 = \angle PDI_1$. Then $AP = AD \cdot \tan \angle ADP = 8\tan(2\theta)$. Since we are given the length $I_1 I_2$, we focus our attention on $\triangle I_1 D I_2$.

Note that both I_1 and I_2 lie on $\overline{AC}$, which bisects both $\angle PAD$ and $\angle BCD$. Furthermore,

$$\angle I_1 D I_2 = \frac{1}{2}(\angle ADP + \angle CDP) = 45°.$$

Let the center of the square be O, which is the midpoint of AC. Note that $\overline{OD}$ is the altitude for the base $I_1 I_2$. Then we have

$$\angle ODI_1 = \angle ODA - \angle ADI_1 = 45° - \theta,$$

and hence

$$\angle ODI_2 = \angle I_1 D I_2 - \angle ODI_2 = 45° - (45° - \theta) = \theta.$$

We will calculate the base over height ratio $\frac{I_1 I_2}{OD}$ in two different ways:

First, since $I_1 I_2 = \frac{7\sqrt{2}}{2}$ and $OD = \frac{BD}{2} = 4\sqrt{2}$, we get $\frac{I_1 I_2}{OD} = \frac{7}{8}$.

We also have

$$\frac{I_1 I_2}{OD} = \frac{OI_1}{OD} + \frac{OI_2}{OD} = \tan(45° - \theta) + \tan(\theta) = \frac{1-t}{1+t} + t = \frac{1+t^2}{1+t},$$

where $t = \tan(\theta)$. Combining the two results, we get

$$\frac{1+t^2}{1+t} = \frac{7}{8} \Rightarrow 8t^2 - 7t + 1 = 0.$$

Solving this quadratic equation yields $t = \frac{7 \pm \sqrt{17}}{16}$. But $\theta < 45°$ because $\angle ADP = 2\theta < 90°$. This implies that $t = \tan\theta < 1$ and we conclude that $t = \frac{7 - \sqrt{17}}{16}$.

Lastly, note that

$$
\begin{aligned}
AP &= 8\tan\angle ADP = 8\tan(2\theta) = \frac{16t}{1-t^2} = 16t \cdot \frac{1}{1-t} \cdot \frac{1}{1+t} \\
&= (7 - \sqrt{17}) \cdot \frac{16}{9 + \sqrt{17}} \cdot \frac{16}{23 - \sqrt{17}} = (7 - \sqrt{17}) \cdot \frac{9 - \sqrt{17}}{4} \cdot \frac{23 + \sqrt{17}}{32} \\
&= \frac{(5 - \sqrt{17})(23 + \sqrt{17})}{8} = \frac{49 - 9\sqrt{17}}{4}.
\end{aligned}
$$

Our final answer is $49 + 9 + 17 + 4 = 79$.

13. A set is said to be *odd-sized* if it contains an odd number of elements. Define the product of a set of numbers to be the product of all its elements. For a set S, let $f(S)$ be the sum of the products of all odd-sized subsets of S. Let N be the sum of $f(T)$ as

T ranges over all odd-sized subsets of $\{1, 2, 3, 4, 5, 6, 7\}$. Find the remainder when N is divided by 1000.

Answer (880): For any set of numbers R, let $\mathrm{prod}(R)$ denote the product of elements of R. It is given that

$$f(S) = \sum_{\substack{T \subseteq S \\ |T| = odd}} \mathrm{prod}(T).$$

Note that $f(R)$ can be written as a difference between products as follows:

$$f(R) = \frac{1}{2} \left(\prod_{a \in R} (1 + a) - \prod_{a \in R} (1 - a) \right).$$

This correctly computes $f(R)$ because the expansions of the two products cancel the terms that are products of an even number of a's, while adding together the products of an odd number of a's.

We want to find

$$N = \sum_{\substack{T \subseteq A \\ |T| = odd}} f(T),$$

where $A = \{1, 2, 3, 4, 5, 6, 7\}$.

Let $c + R = \{c + r \mid r \in R\}$ and $c - R = \{c - r \mid r \in R\}$ for any set of numbers R and real number c. Then we can express the equation above with $f(R)$ as

$$f(R) = \frac{1}{2} \left(\mathrm{prod}(1 + R) - \mathrm{prod}(1 - R) \right).$$

Using the relation above between f and prod, we get

$$N = \sum_{\substack{T\subseteq A \\ |T|=odd}} f(T)$$

$$= \sum_{\substack{T\subseteq A \\ |T|=odd}} \left(\frac{1}{2}\mathrm{prod}(1+T) - \frac{1}{2}\mathrm{prod}(1-T)\right)$$

$$= \frac{1}{2}\sum_{\substack{1+T\subseteq 1+A \\ |1+T|=odd}} \mathrm{prod}(1+T) - \frac{1}{2}\sum_{\substack{1-T\subseteq 1-A \\ |1-T|=odd}} \mathrm{prod}(1-T)$$

$$= \frac{1}{2}f(1+A) - \frac{1}{2}f(1-A)$$

$$= \frac{1}{2}\left(\frac{1}{2}(\mathrm{prod}(1+(1+A))) - \mathrm{prod}(1-(1+A)))\right)$$

$$\quad -\frac{1}{2}\left(\frac{1}{2}(\mathrm{prod}(1+(1-A))) - \mathrm{prod}(1-(1-A)))\right)$$

$$= \frac{1}{4}\left(\mathrm{prod}(2+A) - \mathrm{prod}(-A) - \mathrm{prod}(2-A) + \mathrm{prod}(A)\right)\cdot$$

We now calculate the prod terms above:

$$\begin{aligned}
\mathrm{prod}(A) &= 1\cdot 2\cdots 7 = 5040,\\
\mathrm{prod}(2+A) &= 3\cdot 4\cdots 9 = 181440,\\
\mathrm{prod}(-A) &= (-1)(-2)\cdots(-7) = -5040,\\
\mathrm{prod}(2-A) &= (2-1)(2-2)\cdots(2-7) = 0.
\end{aligned}$$

Plugging these back in the equation above for N, we get

$$N = \frac{1}{4}\left(181440 - (-5040) - 0 + 5040\right) = 47880 \equiv 880 \pmod{1000}.$$

14. Let S be the sum of the squares of the areas of all noncongruent and nondegenerate triangles with integer side lengths and perimeter 30. Find the remainder when S is divided by 1000.

Answer (85): For the sake of non-congruence, let $a \geq b \geq c$ be the sides of such a triangle. We use Ravi Substitution: let $x = s-a$, $y = s-b$, and $z = s-c$, where $s = \frac{a+b+c}{2} = 15$. Then $x \leq y \leq z$ are positive integers satisfying $x+y+z = s = 15$. Furthermore, the square of the area of such a triangle is given by Heron's formula as

$$s(s-a)(s-b)(s-c) = (x+y+z)xyz = 15xyz,$$

so we wish to find the sum

$$S = 15 \sum xyz$$

over positive integers x, y, z such that $x \le y \le z$ and $x + y + z = 15$.

We have $x \le \frac{x+y+z}{3} = 5$. So, we can write $S = 15 \sum_{k=1}^{5} S_k$ where S_k is the sum of such xyz terms where $x = k$. We rewrite S_k as

$$S_k = k \sum yz, \text{ where } k \le y \le z, \text{ and } y + z = 15 - k.$$

We can compute that

- $S_1 = 1 \cdot (1 \cdot 13 + 2 \cdot 12 + 3 \cdot 11 + 4 \cdot 10 + 5 \cdot 9 + 6 \cdot 8 + 7 \cdot 7) = 252,$

- $S_2 = 2 \cdot (2 \cdot 11 + 3 \cdot 10 + 4 \cdot 9 + 5 \cdot 8 + 6 \cdot 7) = 2 \cdot 170 = 340,$

- $S_3 = 3 \cdot (3 \cdot 9 + 4 \cdot 8 + 5 \cdot 7 + 6 \cdot 6) = 3 \cdot 130 = 390,$

- $S_4 = 4 \cdot (4 \cdot 7 + 5 \cdot 6) = 4 \cdot 58 = 232,$

- $S_5 = 5 \cdot (5 \cdot 5) = 125.$

Finally, the value of S is

$$S = 15 \cdot (252 + 340 + 390 + 232 + 125) = 15 \cdot 1339 = 20085 \equiv 85 \pmod{1000}.$$

15. In triangle ABC, circles ω_1 and ω_2 with radii $9\sqrt{3}$ and $3\sqrt{3}$, respectively, are both tangent to each other and side $\overline{BC}$. Moreover, ω_1 is tangent to side $\overline{AB}$ and ω_2 is tangent to side $\overline{AC}$. The common external tangent line $\ell \ne BC$ to both circles intersects line AC at point E and line AB at point F. Given that $EC = 7$ and $FB = 57$, compute the minimum possible value of AF.

Answer (19):

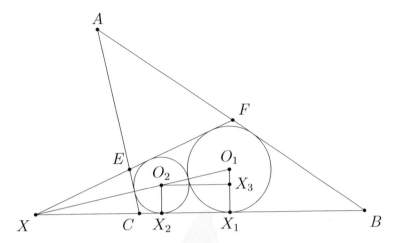

Let X be the intersection of lines EF and BC, and let O_1 and O_2 be the respective centers of ω_1 and ω_2. Then points O_1, O_2, X are collinear. Let the projections of O_1 and O_2 onto line BC be X_1 and X_2, and let the projection of O_2 onto O_1X_1 be X_3. Then $\angle O_1X_3O_2 = 90°$, $O_1X_3 = 6\sqrt{3}$, and $O_1O_2 = 12\sqrt{3}$, implying that $\angle O_1O_2X_3 = 30°$. This, in turn, implies that $\angle EXC = 60°$.

Observe that O_2 is an excenter of $\triangle EXC$. Thus, by excircle rules, $XE + CX + EC = 2XX_2 = 18$ implying that $XE + XC = 11$. Combined with $\angle EXC = 60°$ and using Law of Cosines, we have that $\{EX, XC\} = \{3, 8\}$. Similarly, using that O_1 is the incircle of $\triangle FXB$, we get $\{FX, XB\} = \{48, 63\}$.

By using Menelaus' Theorem on triangle FXB and line AEC, we have that

$$\frac{BA}{AF} \cdot \frac{FE}{EX} \cdot \frac{XC}{CB} = 1.$$

Plugging in $FE = FX - EX$, $CB = BX - XC$, and isolating the AF term, we get

$$1 + \frac{57}{AF} = \frac{\frac{BX}{XC} - 1}{\frac{FX}{EX} - 1}.$$

Among the cases $\{EX, XC\} = \{3, 8\}$, $\{FX, XB\} = \{48, 63\}$, the case $(EX, XC) = (8, 3)$, $(FX, XB) = (48, 63)$ yields the smallest value for AF; in particular, this implies that

$$1 + \frac{57}{AF} = \frac{\frac{63}{3} - 1}{\frac{48}{8} - 1} = 4,$$

and $AF = 19$.

AIME PRACTICE TESTS VOL 1

TEST-4

INSTRUCTIONS

1. This test has 15 questions. All answers are integers ranging from 0 to 999, inclusive. Your score will be the number of correct answers; i.e., there is neither partial credit nor a penalty for wrong answers.

2. No aids other than scratch paper, graph paper, ruler, compass, and protractor are permitted. In particular, calculators are **not** permitted.

3. Figures are not necessarily drawn to scale.

4. You will have **3 hours** to complete the test.

1. Let $A = \{2, 4, 6, 8, 10\}$ and $B = \{1, 3, 5, 7, 9\}$. A number a is chosen from set A, and a number b is chosen from set B. The sum of all values of $\frac{b}{a}$ for every choice of a and b, repeated values included, can be represented as $\frac{m}{n}$, where m and n are relatively prime positive integers. Find $m + n$.

2. Points E and F are on sides $\overline{AB}$ and $\overline{BC}$, respectively, of rectangle $ABCD$. It is given that $\frac{AE}{BE} = 3$ and $\frac{CF}{BF} = 2$. Segments $\overline{DE}$ and $\overline{AF}$ intersect at point G.
The ratio of the area of quadrilateral $EBFG$ to rectangle $ABCD$ can be expressed as $\frac{m}{n}$, where m and n are relatively prime positive integers. Find $m + n$.

3. Consider paths on the coordinate plane from $(0, 8)$ to $(81, 5)$ that pass through $(21, 20)$ and intersect the x-axis. The least possible length of such a path can be expressed in the form $a + b\sqrt{c}$ where a, b, c are positive integers and c is not divisible by the square of any prime. Find $a + b + c$.

4. Let ABC be a triangle and A_1, B_1, C_1 be the midpoints of BC, CA, AB, respectively. It is given that $BB_1 = 450$, $CC_1 = 600$ and $BC = 500$. If D is the foot of the altitude from A, then find DA_1.

5. Find the number of distinct polynomials $P(x)$ with only positive integer coefficients and degree at most five such that $P(1) \leq 9$.
For example $P(x) = x + 1$ is one of these polynomials but $P(x) = x$ is not because its constant term is 0, not a positive integer.

6. Ana, Bob, and Carol are playing a game with the set $S = \{1, 2, \ldots, 10\}$. Ana randomly chooses a subset $\mathcal{S}_1$ of S with size 2, Bob randomly chooses a subset $\mathcal{S}_2$ of S with size 3, and Carol randomly chooses a subset $\mathcal{S}_3$ of S with size 4. Their choices are all independent of each other.
The expected number of elements of S that are not in any of $\mathcal{S}_1, \mathcal{S}_2$, or $\mathcal{S}_3$ can be expressed as $\frac{p}{q}$ where p and q are relatively prime positive integers. Find $p + q$.

7. Given that
$$7^{11} + 11^{13} + 13^7 = 34{,}524{,}\overline{abc}{,}219{,}191$$

for some digits a, b, c, evaluate $100a + 10b + c$.

8. Let $\overline{AB}$ be a diameter of circle ω with radius 10. C and D are points on the line tangent to ω at B, such that B, C, D lie on the line in that order. Let $\overline{AC}$ and $\overline{AD}$ intersect ω again at E and F, respectively, and let $\overline{EF}$ intersect $\overline{CD}$ at G. Let H be a point on segment $\overline{CD}$ such that G is the midpoint of $\overline{BH}$. If $CH = 8$ and $DH = 12$, then find AG^2.

9. Suppose positive real numbers x, y, z satisfy $x + y + z = 1$ and
$$\frac{x + yz}{4} = \frac{y + zx}{6} = \frac{z + xy}{9}.$$

Then if $xy + yz + zx = \frac{m}{n}$ for relatively prime positive integers m and n, compute $m + n$.

10. Find the number of functions f from set $\mathcal{S} = \{1, 2, 3, 4, 5\}$ to itself such that for all $x, y \in \mathcal{S}$,
$$f(f(x)) - f(f(y)) = f(x) - f(y).$$

11. Let ω be a complex number for which
$$z = \frac{\omega - 3}{(2 + 25i)(\omega - 4i)}$$

is a real number. The maximum possible value of $|\omega|$ can be expressed as $\frac{\sqrt{a} + \sqrt{b}}{c}$, where a, b, c are positive integers and a, b are relatively prime. Find the remainder when $a + b + c$ is divided by 1000.

12. For every positive integer n, let $\varphi(n)$ denote the number of positive integers less than or equal to n that are relatively prime to n. If $m = 210$ and

$$S = \sum_{d \mid m^4} \frac{\varphi(d)}{d^2},$$

then find the remainder when $S \cdot m^5$ is divided by 840.

13. A regular 36-gon is inscribed in a circle with radius 1. Let A be a fixed vertex on the 36-gon. Let N be the number of hexagons such that:
(i) one of the vertices is A,
(ii) all of its vertices are among the vertices of the regular 36-gon,
(iii) and all of whose edges have length strictly between $\frac{\sqrt{6}-\sqrt{2}}{2}$ and $\sqrt{2}$.
Find the remainder when N is divided by 1000.

14. The sequence $\{a_k\}$ of real numbers satisfies $a_0 = 1$, $a_1 = \frac{\sqrt{3}}{2}$, and

$$2a_{k+1}a_k - a_{k+1}a_{k-1} + \frac{1}{2}a_k a_{k-1} = -\frac{1}{4^k}$$

for all $k \geq 1$. We can express

$$S = \sum_{k=0}^{\infty} a_k = a_0 + a_1 + \ldots$$

as $\frac{a+\sqrt{b}}{c}$, where a, b, c are positive integers, and a, c are relatively prime. Find $a+b+c$.

15. The angles of tetrahedron $PABC$ satisfy

$$\cos(\angle BPC) = \frac{4}{5}, \quad \cos(\angle CPA) = \frac{12}{13}, \quad \text{and} \quad \cos(\angle APB) = \frac{24}{25}.$$

A sphere with radius 1 is tangent to all four faces of the tetrahedron, and it is tangent to face PAB at X. The length PX can be written in the form $\frac{p\sqrt{q}}{r}$ for positive integers p, q, r where p and r are relatively prime and q is not divisible by the square of any prime. Find the value of $p + q + r$.

Test-4 Answer Key

1. 709

2. 131

3. 133

4. 210

5. 465

6. 109

7. 752

8. 976

9. 24

10. 196

11. 364

12. 743

13. 751

14. 25

15. 138

Test-4 Solutions

1. Let $A = \{2, 4, 6, 8, 10\}$ and $B = \{1, 3, 5, 7, 9\}$. A number a is chosen from set A, and a number b is chosen from set B. The sum of all values of $\frac{b}{a}$ for every choice of a and b, repeated values included, can be represented as $\frac{m}{n}$, where m and n are relatively prime positive integers. Find $m + n$.

   Answer (709): Notice that by summing up all values of $\frac{b}{a}$, we are multiplying every number from set B with the reciprocal of every number from set A. The sum can be represented as

   $$(1 + 3 + 5 + 7 + 9) \cdot \left(\frac{1}{2} + \frac{1}{4} + \frac{1}{6} + \frac{1}{8} + \frac{1}{10} \right).$$

   This can be simplified to

   $$25 \cdot \frac{137}{120} = \frac{685}{24}.$$

   Thus, our final answer is $685 + 24 = 709$.

2. Points E and F are on sides $\overline{AB}$ and $\overline{BC}$, respectively, of rectangle $ABCD$. It is given that $\frac{AE}{BE} = 3$ and $\frac{CF}{BF} = 2$. Segments $\overline{DE}$ and $\overline{AF}$ intersect at point G.

   The ratio of the area of quadrilateral $EBFG$ to rectangle $ABCD$ can be expressed as $\frac{m}{n}$, where m and n are relatively prime positive integers. Find $m + n$.

   Answer (131):

81

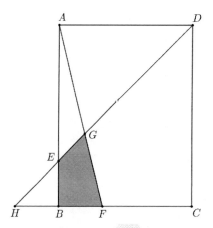

Note that the area $[EBFG]$ is equal to the difference $[ABF] - [AEG]$.

Let lines $\overline{GE}$ and $\overline{BC}$ intersect at H. Then $\triangle BEH$ is similar to $\triangle AED$ by AA similarity. Thus, $\frac{BH}{AD} = \frac{BE}{AE} = \frac{1}{3}$, so $BH = \frac{1}{3}AD$.

Because $\frac{CF}{BF} = 2$, we get $BF = \frac{1}{3}CB = \frac{1}{3}AD$. Thus,

$$HF = HB + BF = \frac{1}{3}AD + \frac{1}{3}AD = \frac{2}{3}AD.$$

Now, observe that $\triangle AGD$ and $\triangle FGH$ are similar by AA similarity with ratio $\frac{DA}{HF} = \frac{3}{2}$. This means that $AG = \frac{3}{5}AF$.

Now, we are ready to compare the area of $EBFG$ to the area of $ABCD$:

$$\begin{aligned}
[EBFG] &= [ABF] - [AEG] \\
&= [ABF] - \frac{AE}{AB} \cdot \frac{AG}{AF} \cdot [ABF] \\
&= [ABF] - \frac{3}{4} \cdot \frac{3}{5} \cdot [ABF] \\
&= \frac{11}{20} \cdot [ABF] \\
&= \frac{11}{20} \cdot \frac{1}{2} \cdot \frac{BF}{BC} \cdot [ABCD] \\
&= \frac{11}{20} \cdot \frac{1}{2} \cdot \frac{1}{3} \cdot [ABCD] \\
&= \frac{11}{120} \cdot [ABCD].
\end{aligned}$$

Thus, our desired ratio is $\frac{11}{120}$, giving a final answer of $11 + 120 = 131$.

3. Consider paths on the coordinate plane from $(0, 8)$ to $(81, 5)$ that pass through $(21, 20)$ and intersect the x-axis. The least possible length of such a path can be expressed in the form $a + b\sqrt{c}$ where a, b, c are positive integers and c is not divisible by the square of any prime. Find $a + b + c$.

Answer (133): Let $A = (0, 8)$, $B = (21, 20)$, and $C = (81, 5)$. Also let $A^* = (0, -8)$ and $C^* = (81, -5)$ be the reflections of A and C along the x-axis. Since we are looking for a shortest path, it must intersect the x-axis only once, let D be this intersection point.

We have two cases depending on which point between B and D is visited first.

Case 1: $A \to D \to B \to C$.
Any such path has length at least

$$
\begin{aligned}
& AD + DB + BC \\
= \ & (A^*D + DB) + BC \\
\geq \ & A^*B + BC \\
= \ & \sqrt{(21 - 0)^2 + (20 - (-8))^2} + \sqrt{(81 - 21)^2 + (20 - 5)^2} \\
= \ & 35 + 15\sqrt{17}.
\end{aligned}
$$

The inequality above follows from the triangle inequality on $\triangle A^*DB$, and the equality is achieved when D lies on the segment $\overline{A^*B}$.

Case 2: $A \to B \to D \to C$.
Similarly, the length of such a path is at least

$$
\begin{aligned}
& AB + BD + DC \\
= \ & AB + (BD + DC^*) \\
\geq \ & AB + BC^* \\
= \ & \sqrt{(21 - 0)^2 + (20 - 8)^2} + \sqrt{(81 - 21)^2 + (-5 - 20)^2} \\
= \ & 3\sqrt{65} + 65.
\end{aligned}
$$

Once again, the inequality above follows from the triangle inequality, this time on $\triangle BDC^*$, and the equality is achieved when D lies on the segment $\overline{BC^*}$.

Finally, to find out which case gives the shortest path, note that

$$
65 + 3\sqrt{65} < 65 + 3 \cdot 10 = 35 + 15 \cdot 4 < 35 + 15\sqrt{17}.
$$

We conclude that the length of the shortest such path is $65 + 3\sqrt{65}$, and the answer is $65 + 3 + 65 = 133$.

4. Let ABC be a triangle and A_1, B_1, C_1 be the midpoints of BC, CA, AB, respectively. It is given that $BB_1 = 450$, $CC_1 = 600$ and $BC = 500$. If D is the foot of the altitude from A, then find DA_1.

Answer (210):

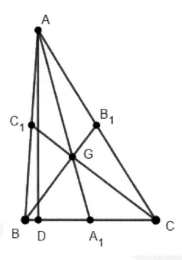

We will find DA_1 using the Pythagorean Theorem on ADA_1.

First, we find AA_1:

Using the fact that the centroid, G, splits the medians in a $2 : 1$ ratio, we find that $BG = \frac{2}{3}BB_1 = 300$ and $CG = \frac{2}{3}CC_1 = 400$. But then, $\triangle BGC$ has side lengths 300, 400, and 500, so $\angle BGC = 90°$, i.e. the two medians are perpendicular. Accordingly, we find that

$$GA_1 = \frac{1}{2}BC = 250 \;\Rightarrow\; AA_1 = 3 \cdot GA_1 = 750.$$

Next, we find AD using areas:

Since $[ABC] = 3 \cdot [BGC]$, we get

$$\frac{1}{2} \cdot BC \cdot AD = 3 \cdot \frac{1}{2} \cdot BG \cdot GC \;\Rightarrow\; \frac{1}{2} \cdot 500 \cdot AD = 3 \cdot \frac{1}{2} \cdot 300 \cdot 400,$$

which gives $AD = 720$.

Finally, using the Pythagorean Theorem on ADA_1, we get

$$DA_1 = \sqrt{AD^2 - AA_1^2} = \sqrt{750^2 - 720^2} = 30\sqrt{25^2 - 24^2} = 30 \cdot 7 = 210.$$

5. Find the number of distinct polynomials $P(x)$ with only positive integer coefficients and degree at most five such that $P(1) \leq 9$.
   For example $P(x) = x + 1$ is one of these polynomials but $P(x) = x$ is not because its constant term is 0, not a positive integer.

   Answer (465): We perform casework on the degree of $P(x)$ and use balls and urns (also known as stars and bars).

   If the degree is 0, the answer is 9.

   If the degree is 1, we see that $P(1) = a + b$ for $P(x) = ax + b$. We want $a + b \leq 9$, where a, b are positive integers. Equivalently, we want $a + b < 10$. Letting g be $10 - (a + b)$ we get $a + b + g = 10$, where a, b, g are positive integers. This gives the result $\binom{9}{2}$ by a balls and urns distribution.

   If the degree is 2, we have $P(1) = a + b + c$ for $P(x) = ax^2 + bx + c$, so once again using a dummy variable $g = 10 - (a + b + c)$ we get $a + b + c + g = 10$ with positive integers a, b, c, g. This has $\binom{9}{3}$ solutions by balls and urns.

   Proceeding in an identical fashion for degrees 3 to 5, we see that each n-degree polynomial has $n + 1$ coefficients and $n + 2$ variables to give a total number of $\binom{9}{n+1}$ polynomials, so the sum of all polynomials of degree between 0 and 5 is

   $$\binom{9}{1} + \binom{9}{2} + \binom{9}{3} + \binom{9}{4} + \binom{9}{5} + \binom{9}{6},$$

   which is equal to $9 + 36 + 84 + 126 + 126 + 84 = 465$.

6. Ana, Bob, and Carol are playing a game with the set $S = \{1, 2, \ldots, 10\}$. Ana randomly chooses a subset $\mathcal{S}_1$ of S with size 2, Bob randomly chooses a subset $\mathcal{S}_2$ of S with size 3, and Carol randomly chooses a subset $\mathcal{S}_3$ of S with size 4. Their choices are all independent of each other.

   The expected number of elements of S that are not in any of $\mathcal{S}_1, \mathcal{S}_2,$ or $\mathcal{S}_3$ can be expressed as $\frac{p}{q}$ where p and q are relatively prime positive integers. Find $p + q$.

   Answer (109): We will use linearity of expectation. For each element, there is a $\frac{10-2}{10}$ chance of not being in $\mathcal{S}_1$, a $\frac{10-3}{10}$ chance of not being in $\mathcal{S}_2$, and a $\frac{10-4}{10}$ chance of not being in $\mathcal{S}_3$. Thus, the probability of not being in any of these three sets is $\frac{8}{10} \cdot \frac{7}{10} \cdot \frac{6}{10} = \frac{42}{125}$. Because there are a total of 10 elements, the expected number of elements not in any of $\mathcal{S}_1, \mathcal{S}_2, \mathcal{S}_3$ is $10 \cdot \frac{42}{125} = \frac{84}{25}$. Thus, the final answer is $84 + 25 = 109$.

7. Given that

$$7^{11} + 11^{13} + 13^7 = 34{,}524{,}\overline{abc}{,}219{,}191$$

for some digits a, b, c, evaluate $100a + 10b + c$.

Answer (752): Let N be the given number. To find $\overline{abc}$, we will find N modulo 1001 in two different ways. We are using modulo 1001 because, when checking the residue of a number modulo 1001, we can take the alternating sum, three digits at a time (since $1000^k \equiv (-1)^k \pmod{1001}$).

On one hand, using Fermat's Little Theorem, we find

$$N \equiv 4^{13} + (-1)^7 \equiv 4 + (-1) \equiv 3 \pmod 7$$
$$N \equiv 7^{11} + 13^7 \equiv 7 + 2^7 \equiv 3 \pmod{11}$$
$$N \equiv 7^{11} + 11^{13} \equiv 7^{-1} + 11 \equiv 0 \pmod{13}.$$

Using the Chinese Remainder Theorem, we first get $N \equiv 3 \pmod{77}$, and then $N \equiv 234 \pmod{1001}$.

On the other hand, we have

$$N \equiv 34 - 524 + \overline{abc} - 219 + 191 \equiv \overline{abc} - 518 \pmod{1001}.$$

Therefore, $\overline{abc} - 518 \equiv 234 \pmod{1001} \Rightarrow \overline{abc} = 752$.

8. Let $\overline{AB}$ be a diameter of circle ω with radius 10. C and D are points on the line tangent to ω at B, such that B, C, D lie on the line in that order. Let $\overline{AC}$ and $\overline{AD}$ intersect ω again at E and F, respectively, and let $\overline{EF}$ intersect $\overline{CD}$ at G. Let H be a point on segment $\overline{CD}$ such that G is the midpoint of $\overline{BH}$. If $CH = 8$ and $DH = 12$, then find AG^2.

Answer (976):

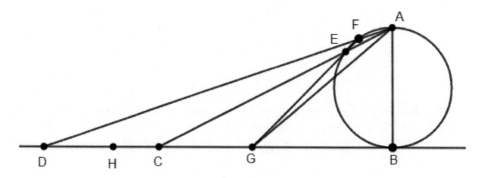

To find AG, we will use Pythagorean Theorem on $\triangle ABG$. We already know that $AB = 2 \cdot 10 = 20$. We proceed to find GB:

First, observe that $\overline{BF}$ and $\overline{BE}$ are altitudes of right triangles ABD and ABC, respectively, so it follows that $\triangle ABD \sim \triangle AFB$ and $\triangle ABC \sim \triangle AEB$. This implies

$$AB^2 = AF \cdot AD = AE \cdot AC.$$

From the last equality, it follows that the points D, C, E, and F lie on a circle, say ω', by the Converse of Power of a Point.

The Power of a Point with respect to point G and circles ω and ω' gives

$$GB^2 = GE \cdot GF = GC \cdot GD.$$

Using $CH = 8$, $HD = 12$, and G being the midpoint of $\overline{BH}$, it follows that

$$GC = GH - CH = GB - 8$$

and

$$GD = GC + CH + HD = (GB - 8) + 8 + 12 = GB + 12.$$

Plugging these in $GB^2 = GC \cdot GD$, we get

$$GB^2 = (GB - 8)(GB + 12),$$

which implies $GB = 24$.

Finally, using the Pythagorean Theorem on $\triangle ABG$, we have that

$$AG^2 = 24^2 + 20^2 = 976.$$

9. Suppose positive real numbers x, y, z satisfy $x + y + z = 1$ and

$$\frac{x + yz}{4} = \frac{y + zx}{6} = \frac{z + xy}{9}.$$

Then if $xy + yz + zx = \frac{m}{n}$ for relatively prime positive integers m and n, compute $m+n$.

Answer (24): Using $x + y + z = 1$, observe that

$$yz + x = yz + x(x + y + z) = (x + y)(x + z).$$

Similarly, we have $zx + y = (y + z)(y + x)$ and $xy + z = (z + x)(z + y)$. Substituting these back in the original equations, we get

$$\frac{(x + y)(x + z)}{4} = \frac{(y + z)(y + x)}{6} = \frac{(z + x)(z + y)}{9}.$$

Dividing $\frac{(x+y)(y+z)(z+x)}{36}$ by all sides, and then summing the numerators and denominators of the fractions, we derive

$$\frac{y+z}{9} = \frac{z+x}{6} = \frac{x+y}{4} = \frac{(y+z)+(z+x)+(x+y)}{9+6+4} = \frac{x+y+z}{9.5}.$$

Now, subtracting the numerators and denominators from those of the last fraction (and doubling the denominators) gives

$$\frac{x}{1} = \frac{y}{7} = \frac{z}{11} = \frac{x+y+z}{1+7+11} = \frac{1}{19}.$$

We conclude that $x = \frac{1}{19}$, $y = \frac{7}{19}$ and $z = \frac{11}{19}$, and finally plugging in the values for x, y, and z gives $xy + yz + zx = \frac{95}{361} = \frac{5}{19}$. So, the answer is $5 + 19 = 24$.

Alternate Solution: Since $x + y + z = 1$, we have

$$x + yz = 1 - y - z + yz = (1-y)(1-z).$$

Similarly, $y + zx = (1-z)(1-x)$ and $z + xy = (1-x)(1-y)$. Then we get

$$\frac{(1-y)(1-z)}{4} = \frac{(1-z)(1-x)}{6} = \frac{(1-x)(1-y)}{9}.$$

Making the substitutions $a = 1 - x$, $b = 1 - y$, $c = 1 - z$, and dividing $\frac{abc}{36}$ by all sides, we find that $a : b : c = 4 : 6 : 9$ with $a + b + c = 3 - (x+y+z) = 2$. Then

$$\frac{a}{4} = \frac{b}{6} = \frac{c}{9} = \frac{a+b+c}{4+6+9} = \frac{2}{19},$$

which gives $a = \frac{18}{19}$, $b = \frac{12}{19}$, and $c = \frac{8}{19}$.

Finally, $x = 1 - a = \frac{1}{19}$, $y = 1 - b = \frac{7}{19}$, $z = 1 - c = \frac{11}{19}$, and $xy + yz + zx = \frac{95}{361} = \frac{5}{19}$, as before.

10. Find the number of functions f from set $\mathcal{S} = \{1, 2, 3, 4, 5\}$ to itself such that for all $x, y \in \mathcal{S}$,

$$f(f(x)) - f(f(y)) = f(x) - f(y).$$

Answer (196): The given condition implies that

$$f(f(x)) - f(x) = f(f(y)) - f(y),$$

so $f(f(c)) - f(c)$ is fixed for all c. Let $k = f(a)$ be the largest element in the range of $f(x)$. Then $f(f(a)) = f(k) \leq f(a)$, and hence

$$f(f(x)) - f(x) = f(f(a)) - f(a) \leq 0.$$

Similarly, letting $m = f(b)$ be the smallest element in the range of $f(x)$, we get

$$f(f(x)) - f(x) = f(f(b)) - f(b) \geq 0.$$

Thus, we get $f(f(x)) = f(x)$ (meaning $f(x)$ is a fixed point of f) for all $x \in \mathcal{S}$.

We will now count the number of functions based on the number of fixed points they have.

Let f have n fixed points, where $n \in \{1, 2, 3, 4, 5\}$. Note that $n > 0$ because, for instance, $f(1)$ is a fixed point of f. The number of ways to choose the n fixed points is $\binom{5}{n}$. For each k among the remaining $5 - n$ values in the domain of f, there are n possible values for $f(k)$ since it must be a fixed point of f.

So, for each $n = 1, 2, 3, 4, 5$, there are $\binom{5}{n} \times n^{5-n}$ possible functions f. Thus, the total number of functions is

$$\sum_{n=1}^{5} \binom{5}{n} \cdot n^{5-n} = 5 \cdot 1^4 + 10 \cdot 2^3 + 10 \cdot 3^2 + 5 \cdot 4^1 + 1 \cdot 5^0 = 196.$$

11. Let ω be a complex number for which

$$z = \frac{\omega - 3}{(2 + 25i)(\omega - 4i)}$$

is a real number. The maximum possible value of $|\omega|$ can be expressed as $\frac{\sqrt{a} + \sqrt{b}}{c}$, where a, b, c are positive integers and a, b are relatively prime. Find the remainder when $a + b + c$ is divided by 1000.

Answer (364): We will interpret this problem geometrically. We are given the condition that

$$\omega - 3 = re^{i\theta}(\omega - 4i),$$

where $re^{i\theta} = c(2 + 25i)$ for some real c, so $\theta = \arctan\left(\frac{25}{2}\right)$. The angle between $\omega - 3$ and $\omega - 4i$ must be θ.

The locus of ω is the set of points P in the complex plane for which the directed angle $\angle APB$ is θ, where $A = 4i$ and $B = 3$ are fixed points. This is a circle that passes through A and B. Let C_1 be this circle, and let O_1 and R be its center and radius, respectively. Then note that $\angle AO_1B = 2\theta$ and since $0 < \theta < 90°$, it follows that O (the origin) and O_1 are on different sides of $\overline{AB}$.

We want the maximum value of $|\omega| = |OP|$. By the triangle inequality on $\triangle OO_1P$, we have $|OP| \leq |OO_1| + |O_1P| = |OO_1| + R$, and equality is achieved when O, O_1, and P are collinear.

Since $\triangle AO_1B$ is isosceles with $AO_1 = BO_1 = R$ and $\angle AO_1B = 2\theta$, we get $AB = 2R\sin\theta$. From $\tan\theta = \frac{25}{2}$ we find that $\sin\theta = \frac{25}{\sqrt{629}}$. Also $AB = 5$. So, we have $R = \frac{\sqrt{629}}{10}$.

Next, we will find $|OO_1|$ using the Law of Cosines on $\triangle OAO_1$:

To find $\cos(\angle OAO_1)$, let $\alpha = \angle OAB$. Then $\angle OAO_1 = \angle OAB + \angle BAO_1 = \alpha + 90 - \theta$. Using $(\cos\alpha, \sin\alpha) = (\frac{4}{5}, \frac{3}{5})$ and $(\cos\theta, \sin\theta) = (\frac{2}{\sqrt{629}}, \frac{25}{\sqrt{629}})$, we get

$$
\begin{aligned}
\cos(\angle OAO_1) &= \cos(\alpha + 90 - \theta) \\
&= \sin(\theta - \alpha) \\
&= \sin\theta\cos\alpha - \sin\alpha\cos\theta \\
&= \frac{25}{\sqrt{629}} \cdot \frac{4}{5} - \frac{3}{5} \cdot \frac{2}{\sqrt{629}} \\
&= \frac{94}{5\sqrt{629}}.
\end{aligned}
$$

Now the Law of Cosines on $\triangle OAO_1$ gives

$$
\begin{aligned}
OO_1^2 &= OA^2 + AO_1^2 - 2OA \cdot AO_1 \cdot \cos(\angle OAO_1) \\
&= 4^2 + R^2 - 2 \cdot 4 \cdot R \cdot \cos(\angle OAO_1) \\
&= 16 + \frac{629}{100} - 2 \cdot 4 \cdot \frac{\sqrt{629}}{10} \cdot \frac{94}{5\sqrt{629}} \\
&= 16 + \frac{629}{100} - \frac{1504}{100} \\
&= \frac{725}{100}.
\end{aligned}
$$

Hence, $OO_1 = \frac{\sqrt{725}}{10}$. The maximum possible value of $|\omega|$ is then $OO_1 + R = \frac{\sqrt{629} + \sqrt{725}}{10}$, and our final answer is $629 + 725 + 10 = 1364 \equiv 364 \pmod{1000}$.

12. For every positive integer n, let $\varphi(n)$ denote the number of positive integers less than or equal to n that are relatively prime to n. If $m = 210$ and

$$
S = \sum_{d \mid m^4} \frac{\varphi(d)}{d^2},
$$

then find the remainder when $S \cdot m^5$ is divided by 840.

Answer (743): Let's define $F : \mathbb{Z}^+ \to \mathbb{R}$ as $F(n) = \sum_{d\,|\,n} \frac{\varphi(d)}{d^2}$. We want to find

$$N = S \cdot m^5 = F(210^4) \cdot 210^5 \quad (\text{mod } 840).$$

To evaluate N, we will first show that F is multiplicative:

Lemma: Because both $\varphi(d)$ and d^2 are multiplicative functions, so is F. It is, $F(ab) = F(a)F(b)$ whenever $gcd(a, b) = 1$.

Proof. The key in the proof below is the bijection between divisors of ab and pairs of divisors of a and b:

$$
\begin{aligned}
F(a)F(b) &= \left(\sum_{d_1\,|\,a} \frac{\varphi(d_1)}{d_1^2} \right) \left(\sum_{d_2\,|\,b} \frac{\varphi(d_2)}{d_2^2} \right) \\
&= \sum_{d_1\,|\,a,\ d_2\,|\,b} \frac{\varphi(d_1)\varphi(d_2)}{d_1^2 d_2^2} \\
&= \sum_{(d_1 d_2)\,|\,ab} \frac{\varphi(d_1 d_2)}{(d_1 d_2)^2} \\
&= \sum_{d\,|\,ab} \frac{\varphi(d)}{d^2} \\
&= F(ab) \quad \square
\end{aligned}
$$

Since F is multiplicative, it follows that

$$F(210^4) = F(2^4)F(3^4)F(5^4)F(7^4).$$

But for a prime number p:

$$
\begin{aligned}
F(p^4) &= 1 + \frac{\varphi(p)}{p^2} + \frac{\varphi(p^2)}{p^4} + \frac{\varphi(p^3)}{p^6} + \frac{\varphi(p^4)}{p^8} \\
&= 1 + \frac{p-1}{p^2} + \frac{p^2-p}{p^4} + \frac{p^3-p^2}{p^6} + \frac{p^4-p^3}{p^8} \\
&= \frac{p^8 + p^7 - p^3}{p^8} = \frac{p^5 + p^4 - 1}{p^5}.
\end{aligned}
$$

Then we find that

$$
\begin{aligned}
N &= F(210^4) \cdot 210^5 \\
&= \left(\prod_{p=2,3,5,7} \frac{p^5 + p^4 - 1}{p^5} \right) 210^5 \\
&= (2^5 + 2^4 - 1)(3^5 + 3^4 - 1)(5^5 + 5^4 - 1)(7^5 + 7^4 - 1).
\end{aligned}
$$

We can evaluate N modulo 840 using the Chinese Remainder Theorem:

Looking at N modulo 3, 5, 7, and 8 we find that the remainders are 2, 3, 1, and 7, respectively. Recombining these, we get $N \equiv 743 \pmod{840}$.

Alternatively, we can find that

$$
\begin{aligned}
N &= (2^5 + 2^4 - 1)(3^5 + 3^4 - 1)(5^5 + 5^4 - 1)(7^5 + 7^4 - 1) \\
&= (47 \cdot 323) \cdot (3749 \cdot 19,207) \\
&\equiv (47 \cdot 323) \cdot (389 \cdot 727) \pmod{840} \\
&\equiv 61 \cdot 563 \pmod{840} \\
&\equiv 743 \pmod{840}.
\end{aligned}
$$

Remark: The lemma is a special case of the following theorem regarding multiplicative functions, which can be proven similarly:

Theorem: Let f be a function defined on positive integers and let F be defined as

$$
F(n) = \sum_{d \mid n} f(d).
$$

Then if f is multiplicative, so is F.

13. A regular 36-gon is inscribed in a circle with radius 1. Let A be a fixed vertex on the 36-gon. Let N be the number of hexagons such that:

(i) one of the vertices is A,

(ii) all of its vertices are among the vertices of the regular 36-gon,

(iii) and all of whose edges have length strictly between $\frac{\sqrt{6} - \sqrt{2}}{2}$ and $\sqrt{2}$.

Find the remainder when N is divided by 1000.

Answer (751): Note that the length condition implies that any two adjacent vertices of the hexagon must differ by a central angle in the unit circle that is strictly between 30 and 90 degrees. Hence, between two adjacent points of the hexagon, there can be 3, 4, 5, 6 or 7 points of the 36-gon.

Starting at A and going clockwise direction, we count the points of the 36-gon. 6 of them appear in the hexagon so 30 of them are in between the vertices of the hexagon. Since there are 6 intervals between points of the hexagon and each interval contain $\{3, 4, 5, 6, 7\}$ points of the 36-gon, we have 6 of these numbers summing to 30. Subtracting 3 from each number, we get 6 numbers among $\{0, 1, 2, 3, 4\}$ summing to 12. So we need to count the number of solutions of $a_1 + \ldots + a_6 = 12$ where $a_i \in \{0, 1, 2, 3, 4\}$.

We will count these using complementary counting and PIE:

For $i = 1, \ldots, 6$, let S_i be the set of integer solutions to the equation

$$\sum_{k=1}^{6} a_k = a_1 + \ldots + a_6 = 12, \text{ where } a_i \geq 5.$$

Then, we want non-negative integer solutions to the equation that are not in any of the S_i's. Note that the intersection of 3 or more S_i's is empty. So, by PIE and symmetry, we have

$$\left| \bigcup_{i=1}^{6} S_i \right| = 6|S_1| - \binom{6}{2}|S_1 \cap S_2|.$$

Using balls and urns, we find that $|S_1| = \binom{12}{5}$ and $|S_1 \cap S_2| = \binom{7}{5}$. Hence, we have

$$\left| \bigcup_{i=1}^{6} S_i \right| = 6\binom{12}{5} - 15\binom{7}{5} = 6 \cdot 792 - 15 \cdot 21 = 4437.$$

Using balls and urns one more time, we find that the number of all non-negative integer solutions is $\binom{17}{5} = 6188$. Hence, the number of desired solutions is $6188 - 4437 = 1751$, whose remainder when divided by 1000 is 751.

14. The sequence $\{a_k\}$ of real numbers satisfies $a_0 = 1$, $a_1 = \frac{\sqrt{3}}{2}$, and

$$2a_{k+1}a_k - a_{k+1}a_{k-1} + \frac{1}{2}a_k a_{k-1} = -\frac{1}{4^k}$$

for all $k \geq 1$. We can express

$$S = \sum_{k=0}^{\infty} a_k = a_0 + a_1 + \ldots$$

as $\frac{a+\sqrt{b}}{c}$, where a, b, c are positive integers, and a, c are relatively prime. Find $a+b+c$.

Answer (25): We first multiply both sides of the recursive sequence equation by 4^k to get

$$2^{2k+1}a_{k+1}a_k - 2^{2k}a_{k+1}a_{k-1} + 2^{2k-1}a_k a_{k-1} = -1.$$

Observe that for each term, the sum of the two subscripts is equal to the exponent of 2, which motivates us to define the sequence $b_k = 2^k a_k$. This sequence b_k satisfies

$$b_{k+1}b_k - b_{k+1}b_{k-1} + b_k b_{k-1} = -1.$$

Solving this for b_{k+1}, we get

$$b_{k+1}(b_k - b_{k-1}) = -(1 + b_k b_{k-1})$$

and

$$b_{k+1} = \frac{1 + b_k b_{k-1}}{b_{k-1} - b_k}.$$

But this is the cotangent subtraction formula. So, if we write $b_0 = \cot(\theta_0)$ and $b_1 = \cot(\theta_1)$, then we will have $b_k = \cot(\theta_k)$ where $\{\theta_k\}$ satisfies the recursion $\theta_k = \theta_{k-1} - \theta_{k-2}$ for $k \geq 2$.

Next, we will find these angles. $b_0 = a_0 = 1 = \cot(45°)$ and $b_1 = 2a_1 = \sqrt{3} = \cot(30°)$. We find the next several terms using the recursion:

k	0	1	2	3	4	5	6	7
θ_k	45°	30°	−15°	−45°	−30°	15°	45°	30°

So, the angles θ_k repeat every 6 terms. Moreover, note that $\theta_{k+3} = -\theta_k$ for all $k \geq 0$. Using this observation and plugging in the values

$$\cot(45°) = 1, \quad \cot(30°) = \sqrt{3}, \quad \text{and} \quad \cot(-15°) = -(2+\sqrt{3}),$$

we find that

$$\begin{aligned}
S &= \sum_{k=0}^{\infty} a_k = \sum_{k=0}^{\infty} \frac{\cot(\theta_k)}{2^k} \\
&= \left(\frac{\cot(\theta_0)}{2^0} + \frac{\cot(\theta_1)}{2^1} + \frac{\cot(\theta_2)}{2^2} \right) \left(1 - \frac{1}{2^3} + \frac{1}{2^6} - \frac{1}{2^9} + \cdots \right). \\
&= \left(1 + \frac{\sqrt{3}}{2} + \frac{-(2+\sqrt{3})}{4} \right) \left(1 - \frac{1}{2^3} + \frac{1}{2^6} - \frac{1}{2^9} + \cdots \right) \\
&= \frac{2+\sqrt{3}}{4} \cdot \frac{1}{1 - \left(\frac{-1}{8} \right)} = \frac{2+\sqrt{3}}{4} \cdot \frac{8}{9} \\
&= \frac{4+\sqrt{12}}{9}.
\end{aligned}$$

Our final answer is $4 + 12 + 9 = 25$.

15. The angles of tetrahedron $PABC$ satisfy

$$\cos(\angle BPC) = \frac{4}{5}, \ \cos(\angle CPA) = \frac{12}{13}, \text{ and } \cos(\angle APB) = \frac{24}{25}.$$

A sphere with radius 1 is tangent to all four faces of the tetrahedron, and it is tangent to face PAB at X. The length PX can be written in the form $\frac{p\sqrt{q}}{r}$ for positive integers p, q, r where p and r are relatively prime and q is not divisible by the square of any prime. Find the value of $p + q + r$.

Answer (138):

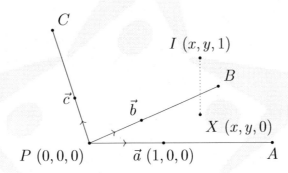

We will use coordinate geometry. Let P be the origin. Orient the space so that A is on the x-axis, and B is on the xy-plane.

Let $\vec{a} = (1, 0, 0)$, $\vec{b} = (b_x, b_y, 0)$, and $\vec{c} = (c_x, c_y, c_z)$ be unit vectors in the directions $\overrightarrow{PA}, \overrightarrow{PB}, \overrightarrow{PC}$, respectively. Without loss of generality, we assume that $b_y > 0$ and $c_z > 0$.

We will find $\vec{b}$ and $\vec{c}$ using the dot product identity:

Recall that for vectors $\vec{u} = (u_x, u_y, u_z)$ and $\vec{v} = (v_x, v_y, v_z)$, their dot product is defined as $\vec{u} \cdot \vec{v} = u_x v_x + u_y v_y + u_z v_z$ and satisfies: $\vec{u} \cdot \vec{v} = |u||v| \cos \alpha$, where α is the angle between $\vec{u}$ and $\vec{v}$.

$$\vec{a} \cdot \vec{b} = (1, 0, 0) \cdot (b_x, b_y, 0) = b_x = \cos \angle APB = \frac{24}{25}.$$

Using this with $|b| = 1$, we get $b_y = \frac{7}{25}$. So, $\vec{b} = \left(\frac{24}{25}, \frac{7}{25}, 0\right)$.

Next, we get

$$\vec{a} \cdot \vec{c} = (1, 0, 0) \cdot (c_x, c_y, c_z) = c_x = \cos \angle APC = \frac{12}{13}.$$

and

$$\vec{b} \cdot \vec{c} = \left(\frac{24}{25}, \frac{7}{25}, 0\right) \cdot (c_x, c_y, c_z) = \frac{24}{25}c_x + \frac{7}{25}c_y = \cos\angle BPC = \frac{4}{5}.$$

Using $c_x = \frac{12}{13}$ this gives us $c_y = -\frac{4}{13}$. Also since $|c| = 1$, we get $c_z = \frac{3}{13}$. Hence, $c = \left(\frac{12}{13}, -\frac{4}{13}, \frac{3}{13}\right)$.

Next, we will use distance formula from a point to a plane to find the center of the sphere. Recall that the distance from a point $Q = (x_0, y_0, z_0)$ to a plane with equation $mx + ny + pz + q = 0$ is $\frac{|mx_0 + ny_0 + pz_0 + q|}{\sqrt{m^2 + n^2 + p^2}}$.

Let $I = (x, y, 1)$ be the center of the unit sphere. Note that its z coordinate is 1 because it is 1 unit away from PAB which lies on the xy-plane.

We have $\text{dist}(I, PAC) = 1$. The PAC plane passes through $P = (0, 0, 0)$, $\vec{a} = (1, 0, 0)$, and $13\vec{c} = (12, -4, 3)$. We find that its equation is $3y + 4z = 0$. Using the distance formula, we get $\frac{|3y+4|}{5} = 1$. Thus, $y = \frac{1}{3}$, because $y > 0$.

We also have $\text{dist}(I, PBC) = 1$. The PBC plane passes through $P = (0, 0, 0)$, $25\vec{b} = (24, 7, 0)$, and $13\vec{c} = (12, -4, 3)$. We find that its equation is $-7x + 24y + 60z = 0$. Then the distance formula gives $\frac{|-7x+24y+60|}{65} = 1$. Plugging in $y = \frac{1}{3}$ we get $|-7x + 68| = 65$. This gives two x solutions which are both positive. To determine which one is the correct one, note that I and $\vec{a} = (1, 0, 0)$ are on the same side of the plane PBC, so they use the same sign with the absolute value. $\text{dist}((1, 0, 0), PBC) = \frac{|-7|}{65} = \frac{-(-7)}{65}$ uses the minus sign, so we get $-(-7x + 68) = 65$, which implies $x = 19$.

We conclude that $I = \left(19, \frac{1}{3}, 1\right)$. Then $X = \left(19, \frac{1}{3}, 0\right)$ and

$$PX = \sqrt{19^2 + \left(\frac{1}{3}\right)^2} = \frac{\sqrt{3250}}{3} = \frac{5\sqrt{130}}{3}.$$

The answer is $5 + 130 + 3 = 138$.

Alternate Solution: We will use trigonometry. First, we will prove three lemmas showing trigonometric identities in 3D.

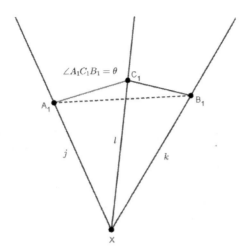

Lemma 1: If three rays, l, j, and k, have a common endpoint, X, meet at angles of α, β, and γ, and form a dihedral angle of θ opposite angle γ, then

$$\cos\alpha\cos\beta + \sin\alpha\sin\beta\cos\theta = \cos\gamma.$$

Proof: Suppose the angle α lies between k and l, β between l and j, and γ between j and k. Let C_1 be on l such that $XC_1 = 1$. Let A_1 and B_1 be on j and k, respectively, such that $\angle XC_1A_1 = \angle XC_1B_1 = 90°$. Then, we know that $\angle A_1C_1B_1 = \theta$. Note that $XA_1 = \sec(\beta)$, $C_1A_1 = \tan(\beta)$, $XB_1 = \sec(\alpha)$, and $C_1B_1 = \tan(\alpha)$. Using Law of Cosines on triangles $A_1C_1B_1$ and A_1XB_1, we find $A_1B_1^2$ in two ways and equate:

$$A_1B_1^2 = XA_1^2 + XB_1^2 - 2XA_1 \cdot XB_1 \cdot \cos\gamma = C_1A_1^2 + C_1B_1^2 - 2C_1A_1 \cdot C_1B_1 \cdot \cos\theta.$$

We substitute lengths for the trigonometric values stated earlier, use the identity

$$\sec^2 v - \tan^2 v = 1,$$

and simplify. The result is $\cos\alpha\cos\beta + \sin\alpha\sin\beta\cos\theta = \cos\gamma$.

Lemma 2: In the configuration stated in Lemma 1, if $\theta = \frac{\pi}{2}$, then $\cos\alpha\cos\beta = \cos\gamma$.

Proof: We substitute $\cos\theta = 0$ into

$$\cos\alpha\cos\beta + \sin\alpha\sin\beta\cos\theta = \cos\gamma.$$

The result is $\cos\alpha\cos\beta = \cos\gamma$.

Lemma 3: In the configuration stated in Lemma 1, if the dihedral angle opposite β has measure $\frac{\pi}{2}$, then $\tan\gamma = \tan\theta\sin\alpha$.

Proof: We start with the equation from Lemma 1, $\cos\alpha\cos\beta + \sin\alpha\sin\beta\cos\theta = \cos\gamma$. Using Lemma 2, we have $\cos\beta = \cos\alpha\cos\gamma$, so we can substitute $\cos\beta = \cos\alpha\cos\gamma$

and also $\sin\beta = \sqrt{1 - \cos^2\alpha\cos^2\gamma}$:

$$\cos\alpha\cos\alpha\cos\gamma + \sin\alpha\sqrt{1 - \cos^2\alpha\cos^2\gamma}\cos\theta = \cos\gamma$$
$$\sin\alpha\sqrt{1 - \cos^2\alpha\cos^2\gamma}\cos\theta = \cos\gamma(1 - \cos^2\alpha)$$
$$\sin\alpha\sqrt{1 - \cos^2\alpha\cos^2\gamma}\cos\theta = \cos\gamma\sin^2\alpha$$
$$\sqrt{1 - \cos^2\alpha\cos^2\gamma}\cos\theta = \cos\gamma\sin\alpha$$
$$(1 - \cos^2\alpha\cos^2\gamma)\cos^2\theta = \cos^2\gamma\sin^2\alpha$$
$$((1 - \cos^2\alpha)\cos^2\gamma + 1 - \cos^2\gamma)\cos^2\theta = \cos^2\gamma\sin^2\alpha$$
$$(\sin^2\alpha\cos^2\gamma + \sin^2\gamma)\cos^2\theta = \cos^2\gamma\sin^2\alpha$$
$$\sin^2\alpha\cos^2\gamma\cos^2\theta + \sin^2\gamma\cos^2\theta = \cos^2\gamma\sin^2\alpha$$
$$\sin^2\gamma\cos^2\theta = \cos^2\gamma\sin^2\alpha(1 - \cos^2\theta)$$
$$\sin^2\gamma\cos^2\theta = \cos^2\gamma\sin^2\alpha\sin^2\theta$$
$$\sin\gamma\cos\theta = \cos\gamma\sin\alpha\sin\theta$$
$$\tan\gamma = \tan\theta\sin\alpha$$

as desired.

Now, we return to the problem. Let I be the incenter of the tetrahedron. We apply Lemma 3 to rays $\overrightarrow{PB}$, $\overrightarrow{PI}$, and $\overrightarrow{PX}$ to find that $\tan\angle IPX = \sin\angle BPX\tan\theta$, where θ is the dihedral angle between planes BPX and BPI. We can find that $\angle BPX$ is equal to $\frac{\angle BPA + \angle BPC - \angle CPA}{2}$ (if you're not sure why, first consider a 2D version of this problem: in triangle ABC, if the incircle is tangent to AB at X, write BX in terms of the sides of the triangle).

Based on this, we use trigonometry sum formulas and half-angle formulas to find that $\sin\angle BPX = \frac{3}{\sqrt{130}}$. Finally, we need to find $\tan\theta$. We know that the dihedral angle between the planes BPX and BPC is 2θ. Because θ is one of the parts bisected by the plane BPI.

Using Lemma 1, we find that $\cos(2\theta) = \frac{12}{13}$. Using the half-angle formulas, we get $\tan(\theta) = \frac{1}{5}$. Now we can put the results together:

$$PX = \frac{IX}{\tan\angle IPX} = \frac{1}{\sin\angle BPX\tan\theta} = \frac{1}{\frac{3}{\sqrt{130}}\cdot\frac{1}{5}} = \frac{5\sqrt{130}}{3}.$$

The answer is $5 + 130 + 3 = 138$.

Made in the USA
Las Vegas, NV
01 December 2024

13057637R00061